EPICURIOUS

THE GREATEST EPICS AND CLASSICS
FROM INDIA AND AROUND THE WORLD

Is there a child ever born who is not curious? So, to capture their imagination, **Sreelata Menon** hopes to not only introduce them to the rich cultural and historical heritage of our inherited past, but also to inspire and tickle their fancy with the magic of our ancient but famous epics.

With more than a dozen books for children to her credit, Sreelata Menon, an unashamed history buff, writes on anything and everything, and can be reached at sreelata0@yahoo.co.in.

EPICURIOUS

THE GREATEST EPICS AND CLASSICS FROM INDIA AND AROUND THE WORLD

SREELATA MENON

illustrated by Sharanya Kunnath

hachette INDIA

First published in 2023 by Hachette India
(Registered name: Hachette Book Publishing India Pvt. Ltd)
An Hachette UK company
www.hachetteindia.com

1

ISBN 978-93-93701-93-0

Hachette Book Publishing India Pvt. Ltd
4th & 5th Floors, Corporate Centre
Plot No. 94, Sector 44, Gurugram – 122003, India

Typeset in Crimson 12.5/16.3
by Manmohan Kumar, Delhi

Printed and bound in India
by Manipal Technologies Limited

MIX
Paper from responsible sources
FSC™ C043100

For Amyra, Liana and Yuvaan,

and all the little people who love adventure

Come aboard the fantasy ship,
There are epic journeys in store;
Sail the oceans of the world,
Join the adventures on the shore;
Greek, Roman, Italian and Indian –
Meet the legendary heroes of yore;
Experience the trials and troubles
Of Achilles, Aeneas, Arjuna and more.
Enjoy a Divine Comedy, go on a tumultuous Odyssey,
Or be witness to a brave and bloody war;
Meet Beowulf, Gilgamesh and the Lion King,
In a universe that will thrill you, yes, to your very core.

CONTENTS

SO...WHAT IS AN EPIC?

Let's say you lived in ancient times and you wanted to narrate a story.

What would you do?

You would choose a suitable hero.

A hero who is more than just brave and heroic. A superhuman who is perhaps part divine.

Someone who undertook long journeys, could fly, sail or traverse land, sea, the underworld and the Heavens; maybe even travel through space and time.

Somebody who could take on supernatural or otherworldly forces like gods, demons, angels, monsters, dragons and super-beasts.

A being who could on occasion, even cheat death.

Yes, someone who could do the most seemingly impossible things and come out blazingly alive, unscathed.

While you are about it, you would also, in a highly stylized and exaggerated poetic style, introduce and combine many mind-boggling stories, myths and legends about your hero and his adventures.

Stories that tell you about right from wrong, victory of good over evil, or simply the rise and fall of nations and civilizations.

You would then narrate these stories with embellished, sometimes over-the-top comparisons that praise your hero or describe his marvellous valour and bravery. Some of these are popular tales; others, as you are the super-creative type, you make up on the spot.

Why do you do it? To give the stories flavour, along with a measure of authenticity, of course.

However, the nicest part is that as you get into your stride, describing the betrayals, wars, love, tragedies and death-defying adventures your hero goes through, you have the freedom to do it not in one verse or two but in thousands and thousands of verses that would run to reams and reams of paper to make up many books...just imagine that!

And lo and behold, you have yourself an epic.

The word 'epic' actually comes from the ancient Greek word *epikos* or *epos* meaning:

- a long, long, really long poetically narrated story,
- with super-duper heroes,
- performing death-defying stunts,
- against demons, beasts and monsters,
- with the help of divine or supernatural forces,

- to enable victory of good over evil,
- using an exaggerated style of word play,
- spanning different worlds, continents or realms,
- and usually starting mid-action with many a flashback.

The many incredible comparisons between ideas or objects that describe this heroism is usually referred to as an 'epic simile' or the 'Homeric tradition' after one of the world's first Greek narrator of epics, Homer.

Now if you were in Europe, you would call upon a Muse to help you, the Muse being a divine creature who gets your creative ideas and juices flowing.

However, if you were in India, you would have a rishi, like Valmiki, teach it to you. You would then unknowingly, go to your father – who doesn't know who you are – and recite it in his court, as Lord Rama's twin sons Lava and Kusha did in the second half of the Ramayana, an Indian epic.

Whether these epics were about real people or just made-up characters in a story is a little difficult to say after all this time, but it is generally accepted that what such poets – yes, they were storytelling poets – sang about had elements of truth in them, exaggerated though these tales might be.

So now that we have established what epics are, there is one other thing you need to know.

Ancient epics came in two forms, in pairs like twins: folk and literary.

The unwritten ones, always recited orally and spread by word of mouth, usually by authors unknown, were popularized as mythology-based folktales. Others, where the poet was generally known since he composed them in the first place, were called literary epics.

Are you thinking, bo-o-o-o-ring?

No, they are actually not so.

Where else would you find bloodthirsty demons and dragons flying about snarling and spouting fire, while gods and demigods helped defend their awesome heroes with equal blood-curdling ferocity?

One point, though. These tales are old and ancient and in the form of poetry.

Why do you need to know about them, let alone read them?

Well, how else would you know about some of the best stories ever told?

Yes, the epics – and there are more than a few from around the globe – can transport you into a world of ultra-adventures that will have you bite your nails in tension, curl your toes in delight and hide your face in fear by the sheer power of their imagery.

Also, how else would you travel through hell and fire to reach paradise, fight devilish monsters to save your kingdom, or even defeat Satan in his evil designs?

Still not convinced? Then imagine ships being tossed about in terrible storms, perilous battles fought back-to-back, the rescue of a queen by soldiers hiding in a wooden horse, or a kingdom being set on fire with a divine *vanara*'s tail – aren't they the very stuff that exciting stories are made of?

The epics are, therefore, not only the earliest collections of legendary or historical events narrated via the exploits of larger-than-life chivalrous heroes who were model human beings, but they are also the earliest form of entertainment known to man.

So, come, enter an ancient world where heroism is a byword, where danger lurks at every corner, where evil is a definite no-no, goodness is a must, duty a done deal and right always right.

BEOWULF

What would you do if your brave warriors were being eaten by monsters and dragons were setting fire to your kingdom?

Grendel lay waiting. In the shadows, lurking in the deep, filthy swamps of great King Hrothgar's kingdom, the beast waited angrily. What made him rage, no one knew. It was perhaps the sound of happiness or the drunken revelry. For the brave men of Denmark had gathered to drink, sup, laugh and tell stories, at the new magnificent hall called Heorot.

As the merriment grew louder and the sounds of laughter spilled over, the monster could hardly contain his fury. Prowling around silently in the dark, he flexed his ugly, gigantic arms restlessly, waiting to pounce.

When all was finally calm and Heorot's happy warriors had settled in for a peaceful night's sleep, he struck.

He went into the hall, broke down the wall, and before the sleeping warriors could gather their wits, with his monstrous teeth he mashed them to pulp and loped away.

For the next few days and every night for all of eleven years thereafter, no less than thirty men and more who sought to fight the beast disappeared from Heorot Hall, leaving behind nothing but some bloodstained floors and pulverized entrails to show that they had lived.

As more and more young warriors lost their lives trying to kill the beast, old King Hrothgar grew sadder and wearier by the year.

Finally came a day when there were no more warriors to brave the night or fight the vicious beast. Yet the monster came, angrier than ever, prowling around, searching for men to eat.

With no one to stop him, his notoriety spread far and wide.

Until one day, a tall fair-headed youth along with fifteen men washed up on the shores of Denmark to take on the monstrous monster and save old King Hrothgar's kingdom.

Who was that youth?

He was Beowulf. A killer of monsters, and he came from the kingdom of Geating (present-day Sweden).

Many years ago, Beowulf's father had sought refuge in King Hrothgar's court when his life and family were in danger. King Hrothgar had been kind and had given them shelter till the danger had passed. It was a kindness Beowulf had never forgotten.

So, Beowulf had asked his uncle Hygelac, who was Geating's king, 'May I go to Hrothgar's help, sire? For he did once save my father and me. His kingdom today is being terrorized by a fiendish beast and his brave warriors are being decimated one by one.'

Thereafter, with his uncle's blessings and his band of courageous soldiers, Beowulf had sailed the rough seas and weathered perilous storms to fetch upon the shores of King Hrothgar's kingdom.

Hrothgar's eyes lit up with relief and joy as he welcomed the blue-eyed giant of a man who had come from afar to help him.

That night, while everyone else retired to sleep, Beowulf and his men lay sleepless in Heorot with swords drawn, waiting to strike at Grendel.

●●●

Grendel came. He prowled around. To his glee, he found more men to feast upon.

With a horrendous growl, he broke through the wall again and before the drawn swords could strike him down, picked up a man and swallowed him whole.

He then moved towards Beowulf.

Quick on his feet, Grendel lifted Beowulf up, but so fast did Beowulf – who was waiting for Grendel – have him in an arm lock so strong that the beast could neither move and loosen Beowulf's hold nor escape.

Roaring maniacally, Grendel twisted and turned. Beowulf simply gripped him tighter and tighter.

Grendel, then, with one mighty push, tried to flee, only to have his enormous arm and shoulder ripped apart.

Dripping blood and whimpering in pain, the grotesque beast that had killed all of Denmark's warriors limped away to die in the dark, filthy swamp that was his home.

With nothing but his bare fists, valiant Beowulf, believed to have the strength of thirty men, thus managed to kill the monstrous beast.

With Grendel's severed arm hung like a trophy high on the wall, there was great happiness in Heorot Hall that night.

●●●

Sadly, however, no one was aware that Grendel had a mother, more ferocious and wicked than Grendel – and she came roaring the following night to avenge her son's death. She picked up Aeschere, one of Hrothgar's closest advisers, and ripped him apart with her horrible teeth. Then she took Grendel's lifeless arm and disappeared, engulfing the kingdom in sorrow once more.

So, holding aloft his huge and trusted sword, Beowulf dived into the dangerous swamp caves under the seas below, fighting off terrifying sea monsters and poisonous sea snakes to ferret out the she-monster from her hiding place

A great battle followed.

However, Beowulf's sword was of no use, nor was the powerful blade that Unferth, the bravest of Hrothgar's braves, had given him. They broke upon Grendel's mother's back.

On the cave's roof, just in time, Beowulf spied an enormous gold-tipped sword. Pouncing upon it, he brought it down on Grendel's mother's head and killed her on the spot.

Finding Grendel lying dead in her lair with his arm beside him, Beowulf lopped off his head too.

Carrying both heads and the arm, Beowulf swam up to the surface of the waters where his men waited anxiously.

A thunderous cheer rent the air. Hrothgar's people knew they were finally rid of the gruesome fiend that had devoured their men.

Presenting King Hrothgar with Grendel's head and the jewelled hilt of the sword that had killed Grendel's mother, Beowulf said, 'Sire, my work here is done. I need to go home.'

A grateful Hrothgar plied him with great riches and gifts, and sent him on his way.

●●●

Fifty years then passed.

Geating had a new king, Hygelac's son. However, he was killed in battle and the crown passed to Beowulf who ruled wisely and well.

His fame as a mighty hero who could take on monsters with his fists had spread like the wind. There was none more heroic or brave across all the seas than Geating's valiant ruler, Beowulf.

Then, one day, among the dangerous gorges under the seas, many, many fathoms deep, a fiery, winged dragon was woken up in his lair.

For three hundred years and more he had lain over a colossal old treasure, undisturbed. Suddenly, a fleeing robber from Beowulf's land had stumbled upon the glittering riches and tried to steal them away.

So, on the trail of his stolen hoard, the dragon rose up in fury to set Beowulf's kingdom and his men on fire.

Quick to rise to the occasion, Beowulf, now an old man, went to fight him on his own, much against the advice of his men.

'I am your king and it is my duty,' he said, before he plunged into the sea, in search of the fierce dragon who could snuff out more lives than you could count.

As his men waited anxiously by the shore, Beowulf fought the final battle of his life.

Thwarting the fire-spitting dragon's every move, Beowulf struck again and again. Alas, his sword melted and he was left to fight with his bare hands – hands that were now weak with age.

Seizing the opportunity, the angry dragon sank his red-hot teeth into Beowulf's neck.

Then, to Beowulf's aid came the warrior Wiglaf, unwilling to leave his king to fight the beast alone. With a single blow, he finished off what his king had begun. And the once-flaming dragon lay as dead as a stone.

Grievously wounded, and knowing he was about to die, Beowulf handed over his crown to Wiglaf. 'Since you braved the waves to come to my rescue, Wiglaf, you

WHO WROTE IT AND WHY

The author of Beowulf is unknown. This eleventh-century Anglo-Saxon folk epic of 3,182 lines in poetic Olde English is a tale of chivalry and courage, and the victory of good over evil, with a superhuman brave hero as a role model. Set in Scandinavia, Beowulf is possibly the oldest surviving long poem in Olde English. The Anglo-Saxons were migrants from northern Europe who settled in England in the fifth and sixth centuries.

His Muse: The Listener.

and you alone have the right to be King of the Geats,' he said.

Then, with his grieving countrymen gathered around, a victorious Beowulf, tired and bleeding, passed away.

Burying him along with his ashes and treasures, his men built him a grand memorial on a mound so high that it stood like a beacon for all others to admire.

His fame and glory had spread through all of Scandinavia. And so, wherever men assembled, as they usually did, they would with awe recount again and again the many valorous deeds of brave King Beowulf the Dragon-slayer.

Archaeologists have dug up what they think is a grave with treasures similar to that of Beowulf, in Sutton Hoo, UK.

PARADISE LOST

God is in His Heaven, but what about Satan? A clash of the Titans and it's all happening in...

Long, long ago, a really long time before the beginning of time, the world was a different place.

It had Heaven above and Hell below, with Chaos in between.

Archangels Gabriel and Michael guarded the gates of Heaven while Sin and Death stood at Hell's door.

Then a mighty war took place in Heaven between God and one of His main angels, Satan.

Satan felt he would rather be a king in Hell than a servant in Heaven.

So, caused by Satan's misplaced pride, the battle raged on for three whole days.

On the first day, God's forces, led by Gabriel and Michael, had the upper hand. On the second day, however, Satan's forces of rebel-angels appeared to be winning.

Then, the Son of God let loose a barrage of thunderbolts and lightning from which there was no escape, and Satan and his forces were jettisoned out of Heaven.

Satan fell. Down, down and down he went.

When he woke up, Satan found himself in Hell. In chains. Amidst a fiery, bubbling and hissing molten lake that was 'spreading darkness instead of light.' And around him lay his forces in complete disarray.

What did God do then?

In five days, He created Earth – dangling on a gold chain from Heaven – with her land, seas, planets, stars, plants, animals and more.

On the sixth day, He fashioned Man out of clay in His own image, breathed life into him and produced Adam, the first man in the world.

Since Adam was lonely, out of Adam's rib God created Eve, the first woman on Earth.

He then threw in a Paradise, with a Garden of Eden and a Tree of Knowledge, laden with fruits so that they might live happily ever after.

However, He told Adam and Eve firmly, 'You are free to do whatever you want, but you are forbidden to eat the fruit of this tree.'

Why did God do all this?

So that the best among this new race, Mankind, could replace Satan and his rebel-angels who had been thrown out of Heaven.

On the seventh day, His work done, God rested.

However, it was not going to be all that easy.

Realizing where he had landed, Satan was livid.

He called a gathering of all the rebel-angels who had been kicked out of Heaven, and there were many.

They met in Pandemonium, their new capital city made of gold in Hell, hastily built on top of a fiery volcano by the fallen angels, supervised by Mammon.

Satan wanted revenge.

'Let's go back and fight God again,' said Moloch, one of the fallen angels.

'No,' argued Beliac, another fallen angel. 'We need to resolve matters peacefully.'

Beelzebub, Satan's able lieutenant, then suggested, 'Hasn't God proved He is all-powerful? We need to tackle God another way. Go to Earth, scope the place and meet this new couple He has created. Though Man is now God's favourite creation, it appears he is not as powerful as the angels.'

Then, proposed Satan, thrilled at the idea of avenging his defeat and humiliation, 'Let us try and corrupt him or turn God's good work into evil and destroy them.'

'Yes,' nodded the others, banging their weapons in complete agreement. 'It's a plan.'

However, who was to go?

'I will,' volunteered Satan immediately.

He was still smarting at how God had wanted him to bow before the Son of God when he, Satan, was the most important angel in all of Heaven.

Wasn't that why he had rebelled?

So, Satan bade his daughter Sin and son Death goodbye at the gates of Hell, even though he knew they were bound to follow him, and made his way up through dark and dreary Chaos to the newly formed Earth.

Disguising himself as a cherub or an angelic winged baby, he innocently asked the Archangel Uriel, 'May I admire God's amazing creations?' and thus entered the Garden of Eden.

Satan then wandered around, amazed at the beauty of the place.

Spotting Adam and Eve frolicking in the Garden, he muttered to himself, 'They seem so happy,' momentarily wishing he hadn't fought with God and got thrown out of Heaven.

Then he remembered why that had happened and turned livid with hate again.

Undecided, he watched them for a while.

When he overheard them talking about the Forbidden Fruit in the Garden of Eden, he realized instantly how to get back at God.

'I will persuade them to disobey God and eat the Forbidden Fruit, and thus avenge myself,' he decided.

So, he turned himself into a toad and hopped across to Eve to ask her, 'Why aren't you eating the fruit on the tree? It's very tasty. I have tried it.'

Uriel, who was close by, watching, suddenly realized who the toad was and rushed to inform Gabriel.

'It's Satan, it's Satan,' he cried, and Gabriel immediately forced Satan to leave the Garden of Eden.

God, realizing that Satan wasn't going to stay away, told the angel Raphael, 'Go warn them about Satan's evil designs.'

So, to Adam and Eve went Raphael, and told them about the rebellion and the terrible war. He cautioned them to beware of Satan, now that they knew why he had been thrown out.

Then God, again aware of what was going to happen, said, 'If Satan succeeds in his evil ways and Adam and Eve disobey my orders, as they are sure to, someone will have to go down to Earth to protect them and take upon himself their sins.'

To God's relief, the Son of God offered to be born as a mortal and take on the sins of mankind.

Satan, meanwhile, unable but determined to get into the Garden of Eden again, circled Earth for seven days and nights. He finally slipped into Paradise through an underground river, first in the form of mist and then as a bird.

After this, he turned himself into a serpent and slithered along among the rose bushes to Eve who was alone.

He then spoke to Eve, who was surprised to hear a serpent speak.

'I have eaten the fruit,' the serpent told her, 'that's why I can speak. Do taste the fruit. It will be good for you too.'

Eve was tempted and despite Adam warning her not to, she bit into the fruit. It was just as God had predicted.

Feeling instantly guilty and ashamed, Eve quickly told Adam what she had done.

A shocked Adam knew she would be punished.

However, he didn't want her to be punished alone.

So, he too took a bite of the Forbidden Fruit.

Thrilled, Satan went chortling back to Hell.

'We can now start to build a bridge from Hell to Earth,' said a delighted Sin and Death.

God, however, was not done with Satan.

Since he went to tempt Eve as a serpent, the moment he reached Hell, Satan found himself turned into a serpent.

So did all the other fallen angels.

'That is their punishment,' God decreed, 'to hiss and slither on their bellies for ever more.'

Then, for having disobeyed God and tasted the fruit, the Son of God showed Adam and Eve a vision of all that was physically in store for them, the pain and suffering that was awaiting them.

Mankind would not only now have to face evil, sin and death but would also be prone to poverty, misery, wars and more suffering.

Adam and Eve were dismayed. Their joy vanished and they began to turn on each other.

They realized their personalities were changing and not for the better.

So, a saddened and repentant Adam and Eve begged the Son of God, 'Please forgive us.'

God, on the advice of His Son, decided to forgive them – partially.

He said, 'If your repentance is true, you will be shown mercy. However, since both of you disobeyed me, you can no longer stay in the Garden of Eden or even in Paradise.'

'Michael,' He called out to the archangel, 'please escort them out and show them what the future will hold for them and for the world.'

WHO WROTE IT AND WHY

John Milton, in 1667 CE, filled ten books with 10,565 lines of English verse as he believed God was eternal and the fall of humankind into sin and death was all a part of God's greater plan. In 1674, his work was reorganized into twelve books. For the most part, he had lost his sight when he composed it. Its sequel *Paradise Regained*, comprising four books of 2,065 lines, deals with Satan trying to tempt Christ, the Son of God. Milton was a prolific writer, and has many poetry, drama (sixteen) and prose (twenty-eight) works to his credit.

Born on 9 December 1608 in London, Milton had initially wanted to become a clergyman. Taught by private tutors from an early age, he studied at St. Paul's School, London, and, in 1632, graduated from Christ College, Cambridge. Proficient in Latin, Greek and other classical languages, he was soon producing poems in all three languages. Having spent some time travelling around Europe, he became very active in literary circles and in a period of much political and religious upheaval, Milton became internationally renowned for defending the right to the freedom of speech and of the press by producing his famous 'pamphlets' of 1644. He began *Paradise Lost* in 1658 and completed it by 1667. Known to have introduced new words from Latin and Greek to the English language, he is considered one of England's greatest poets. Milton died on the 8 November 1674 in London.

His other notable works: *Lycidas* (1637), a pastoral elegy; *Areopagitica,* a speech opposing censorship (1644); *Poems* (1645), a collection of poems; and *Samson Agonistes* (1671), a play.

His Muse: The Holy Spirit.

So, Michael narrated what was actually to come, the history of mankind that was to be and how the Son of God, Jesus, would eventually come down to Earth to save them.

In short, the story of the Bible.

Grateful that they would eventually be saved, Adam held Eve's hand and together they sadly left Eden forever.

And that, according to John Milton, was how Paradise was Lost.

Paradise Lost *was once bound as a book in human skin – that of George Cudmore, a murderer.*

THE DIVINE COMEDY

Where do you think the dead go after they die?

Dante was nine years old when he fell in love. Her name was Beatrice, and she was eight. On a beautiful day in May, when the city of Florence was awash with spring flowers, he lost his little heart to her forever. Too shy to speak, he just stood and watched her laugh and play that day.

Though he looked for her often, it was to be many years before he heard her even speak and as many as nine years more till they exchanged greetings.

That, however, didn't prevent him from loving her deeply from afar.

Then one day, Dante fell seriously ill. In a hazy dream, he saw Beatrice again. She was dying and everyone wept, as did he. He saw her body lying on a couch, and her soul, as light as a cloud, pass through darkness and Hell.

Heartbroken at the very thought of a world without his lady love, he was relieved that it was only a dream.

However, a few days later, it so happened that Beatrice actually passed away.

Inconsolable, Dante had another vision, which brought him peace and calm. He saw a happy Beatrice among angels in Paradise, more radiant than she had ever been on Earth.

No longer sad, Dante wondered what the afterlife might hold, and decided to write what he thought would happen after he died.

He imagined waking up from a deep slumber in a menacing, dark and dense forest at the foot of a huge sunlit mountain. As he tried to make his way through the darkness, a leopard, a ferocious lion and a snarling, hungry she-wolf blocked his path and accosted him. Petrified, he didn't know what to do. If he turned back, he might die in the deep forest. If he went forward, the animals would get him.

Terrified, he hesitated. However, help was near. Virgil, the famous Roman poet Dante so admired, came to his aid. 'Virgil is my hero, but he died long before I was born,' remembered Dante. He nevertheless pleaded, 'Please help me, sir.'

'I will help you,' said Virgil, 'but are you prepared to go through Inferno or Hell where wrongdoers from Earth are punished, and after that through Purgatory where repentant sinners are purified, to finally reach Paradise where God resides?'

'Yes,' nodded Dante, eagerly. 'I am willing to do anything to reach Paradise.'

'Then follow me,' said Virgil and added, 'actually, it was a lovely lady in Paradise who sent me to help you.'

Dante was stunned. 'It must be Beatrice,' he decided. 'Even after having been gone ten long years, she knows of my love for her.'

INFERNO

Delighted yet fearful, Dante thus began his journey into his afterlife, even while he was alive.

Through the frightening forest, avoiding the three animals, Virgil led a scared Dante to the gates of Inferno. Above them hung a sign directing only those who had lost all hope to enter. Then through nine fiery circles of sinners, he steered him to the centre where a snarling Satan waited for those sinners who had no hope. These circles were full of real people – intellectuals, rulers, advisers, popes, friends and enemies – some of whom Dante knew personally. They had been allotted to each circle depending on the degree of sins or crimes they had committed on Earth.

So then, shall we go see what they are?

Avoiding a sea of wailing souls, some of whom Dante recognized, first to Acheron (the River of Woe), they went where Charon, the sullen white-haired cosmic boatman rowed them across, leaving behind suffering souls who – as they were neither fully good nor fully

bad – were unable to enter Hell or Heaven, or be cleansed by Purgatory.

Then as the earth shook violently, Dante was flung on to the opposite shore. A huge, dark, bottomless pit yawned before him. Clinging to Virgil, he entered Inferno's **Circle One** where the souls of all non-believers were held. Banned from entering Heaven due to their lack of faith in God, they were not sent into deep Hell either as they were not actual wrongdoers. They hung in Limbo – in neither Hell nor Heaven.

At **Circle Two**, Dante met a frightening half-beast Minos, who decided which sinner went where, by the number of lashes he handed out with his ugly tail. With two lashes, it was into Circle Two for those who indulged in lust or selfish pleasure. Their punishment – to be buffeted and thrown around violently without rest in a brutal, never-ending storm.

Circle Three was for those who overindulged in food, the gluttons. Forced to lie in cold mud and sleet in heavy rain, they were constantly clawed and bitten by a snapping, three-headed giant dog, Cerberus.

On to **Circle Four**, ruled by Plutus, the god of wealth, where greedy spirits, misers and spendthrifts were punished by being made to push, shove and stone each other endlessly.

Circle Five went past a boiling well on to the swampy River Styx filled with wrathful, fighting naked spirits, who were once people guilty of arrogance and pride. Then, they went to the foot of a tower where Phlegyas, an angry boatman, rowed them across the swamp to the City of Dis which was…

Circle Six, with horrifying demons and the three Furies hanging from its turrets, one of whom was the Gorgon Medusa who could turn you into stone. Filled with the spirits of heretics or those who spoke against God and rulers, they were trapped in red-hot iron tombs heated according to the gravity of the sins of heresy they had committed.

They then reached **Circle Seven**, which was guarded by the monster Minotaur and where armed Centaurs – creatures who were half-man and half-horse – patrolled the banks of a boiling Phlegethon (the River of Blood) and shot arrows at the different types of violent sinners immersed in it.

Passing trees haunted by souls who had killed themselves, Dante and Virgil saw many naked spirits writhing in pain on burning sands. There were flames above and the spirits were weighed down by money purses. The two escaped from there with the help of Geryon, who was man, beast and serpent in one, to Malebolge or evil pit into...

Circle Eight, with its ten concentric ditches, each filled with different kinds of fraudsters – hypocrites, fraudulent priests, thieves, magicians, liars and swindlers. They were being whipped, boiled, burnt or stabbed by turns.

Carried by Virgil over a precipice into **Circle Nine**, a dispirited Dante next spied traitors encased in ice for their treachery, buried in varying postures for having betrayed their family, lords or king and country.

Finally, at the very centre in **Cocytus**, the lake of ice (the River of Wailing), sat the six-winged, three-faced Satan. Weeping blood from his six eyes, he scratched and chewed on the heads of evil men like Judas who had betrayed Jesus Christ.

Virgil quickly climbed over Satan's frozen back and, from the centre of the Earth, clambered up with a demoralized Dante into the open, to reach the outskirts of Purgatory.

PURGATORY

A bright, star-studded blue sky after the gloom of Inferno filled Dante's heart with hope once again.

Cato, a famous writer, suddenly appeared.

Astonished that they had come through Inferno unscathed, he said, 'Virgil, you must tie a green reed around Dante's waist to show his humility and clean his face of all Inferno's muck.' He allowed them to enter the Ante (area before) Purgatory that he guarded – but only after Virgil told him that they were on this journey to Paradise on Beatrice's orders.

Just then a boatload of penitent sinners appeared in a boat, one of whom – Casella – Dante knew and tried to embrace, but could not as Casella was now a spirit who began to sing a haunting melody.

'Don't tarry, move on,' ordered Cato, and so they did. Going up a narrow spiral route, they met white-robed repentant or excommunicated souls cast out for their anti-religious views, among whom was Manfred, King of Naples and Sicily, whom Dante recognized. Then came the spirits of the Indolent Ones or the lazy, who awaited their turn to be allowed up. These were the remorseful, 'last-minute' repenting souls who recounted the story of how the warrior Bonconte Montefeltro narrowly escaped Hell by his last-minute penitence. They begged Dante to intercede on their behalf and tell their relatives to pray for them so that they might enter Purgatory faster. Next was the spirit of the great poet Sordello with whom Dante excitedly argued about all that was wrong with Florence. Sordello now guided them to the lovely Valley of Flowers for the night, where famous, contrite rulers of the past also waited, among whom was Nino Visconti, yet another old friend of Dante's.

Dreaming of being carried heavenward by an eagle with golden feathers, Dante woke up to find himself at the actual gates of Purgatory. Virgil told him, 'No, it wasn't a dream. St. Lucia, an angel, carried you up.' The angel then marked seven Ps for 'P' in *peccato* (sin in Italian) on Dante's forehead as they would encounter **Seven Terraces** or Sins before they reached the top of Purgatory.

Virgil guided Dante on to the first terrace. Carved out of the slopes were the statues of humility, of the Virgin Mary, King David and Emperor Trajan. Before them, being cleansed of the sin of **Pride** or arrogance, carrying heavy weights around their necks, crawling along, unable to stand straight, were many whom Dante knew, those who had once been proud and arrogant. They now warned him against being proud. An angel brushed past him and Virgil told Dante that the first P had been wiped off.

The next stop was **Envy** or jealousy, Wearing sackcloth with their eyelids stitched up, the penitents helped each other along the path. They were being taught humility. Sapia, a woman, told Dante how she had gloated over the defeat of her people in battle and so was being punished. His second P was brushed off.

Moving on to **Wrath** or anger, Dante saw contrite spirits being made to wander around in an unpleasant mist. He had visions of Virgin Mary with the boy Jesus, a weeping woman and St. Stephen, the first Christian martyr, being stoned to death. He also had a discussion with penitents on the roles of emperors and popes. An angel brushed off his third P.

They then reached **Sloth** or laziness, where they were accosted by a sea of repenting spirits who were being made to run non-stop. Virgil told Dante this was due to either a lack of or too much of love, which was also the cause of all sins. Next, Dante dreamed of a terrible, evil temptress or siren and when Virgil woke him at dawn, an angel wiped out the fourth P.

Next was **Avarice** or greed. Weeping penitents chained to the ground were made to lie face down. Dante heard the stories of generous souls, including that of Pope Adrian, all of whom came undone because of greed. Soon, the fifth P disappeared. The mountain suddenly shook violently as the spirit of Statius, a nobleman, punished not for avarice but because he was irreligious, was released after 500 years to meet Virgil, his hero.

They then moved on to **Gluttony** or greed for food, and the sixth P was erased. They went past a fruit-laden tree that warned them of gluttony; here they saw hungry, thirsty, weeping, gaunt, skeleton-like wraiths. Dante was surprised to see a recently dead friend so near the top of the Purgatory Hill and the spirit told him that the man's jump-up was due to his wife's prayers.

And finally, having talked about the nature of the soul and its faculties, how they were created and what happened when a person died, they reached the **seventh terrace**, where those who had indulged in sinful pleasure or **Lust** were being purged in a huge fire.

Dante hesitated, scared to go through more fire.

Virgil then reminded him that he must go through it if he wanted to see Beatrice. To the amazement of the spirits, they passed through the fire, and as night fell soon, they slept on the steps. At dawn, they went to the top of the stairs and finally reached the peak of **Purgatory**.

What a lovely sight greeted them there; it was like an enchanted forest.

Virgil then told him, 'This is as far as I can go. I must return to Limbo. So here I will bid you goodbye.'

Dante, struck by the beauty of the mountaintop, was now hailed by a lovely lady, Matilda, who was plucking flowers.

She took him across a clear stream. 'You are in the **Garden of Eden**,' she said. 'Here, God's creation is still pure and uncorrupted.'

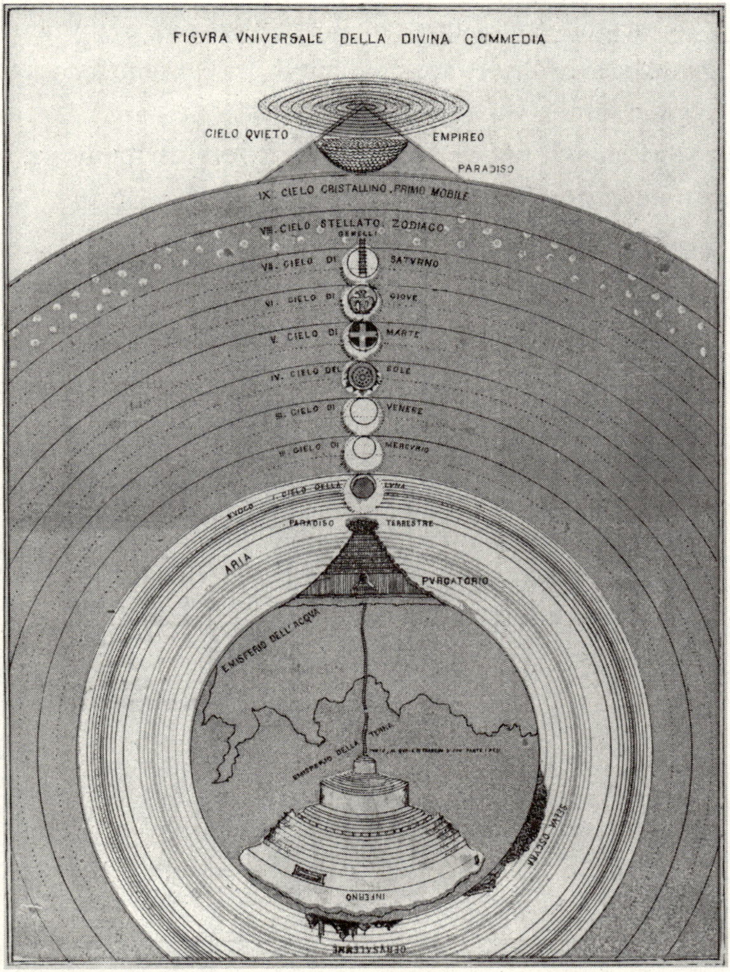

Overview of the Divine Comedy, 1855, one of the series of topographic maps designed by Italian scholar and political figure Michelangelo Caetani to help students understand the epic

A magnificent Christian procession passed by and Dante was thrilled to see a radiant Beatrice come forward to greet him.

Beatrice, however, scolded him for his many past sins and 'for not being religious enough'.

Tearfully, Dante said, 'I'm sorry.'

Next, Matilda took him into the **River Lethe** to wash away his sins and join the procession.

However, when the chariot of the church overturned and was damaged, Beatrice told him, 'Record whatever you see here in your mind. Write it all down when you get back home. A deliverer will soon be born to right any wrongs committed against the Church.'

Dante then took a dip in the **River Enou** to purify himself once more and, then, it was off to Paradise.

PARADISE

Soon, Dante, not quite knowing how he reached there, found himself with Beatrice above the dazzle of the Sun.

Earth looked small and quite far away as Beatrice guided him through Paradise.

Paradise has nine brilliant spheres or heavens, she told him, and to get to its core, he had to go through them all.

So, he first went past a glowing realm of fire and entered the **first heaven, Moon**. It was the home of those spirits – like nuns – who knowingly or unknowingly broke their words or vows.

Giving him a quick run-through of the structure of the universe, Beatrice moved them on to the next, **Mercury**, where souls who carried out good deeds because they desired fame flitted about. They met one such soul, the famous emperor Justinian, who narrated to them a short history of ancient Rome.

Then they went on to **Venus** where happiness reigned, and met the Hungarian king, Charles Martel of Anjou, who explained the need to include all kinds of people while doing good, and to do good out of only love and no other reason.

It was on to the **Sun** next, the sphere of the wise where souls like St. Thomas Aquinas told Dante how important it was not to make hasty judgements and why prudence was a virtue. He then spoke of love and related the story of St. Francis of Assisi and his fall into poverty.

Then came **Mars**, which had the spirits of those who had fought and died for their religion, Christianity. Dante was delighted to meet his great-great-grandfather there, who told him all about himself and the glorious past of the city of Florence. Predicting Dante's future, he said, 'You will be exiled from Florence because of what you write,' and Dante was saddened to hear that.

He found that Beatrice had quickly moved them on to the next heaven of **Jupiter**, which was like a gold-edged silver disc where spirits flew about, joyously creating images and letters akin to birds. 'Was it God?' Dante wondered for a moment when he spied a huge eagle on whose brow sat great emperors and judges like Constantine and Trajan, and others known for their sense of fair justice.

Listening to the song of divine justice from the eagle in Jupiter, they went next to the heaven of **Saturn**. In the centre there, was a ladder of spirits so high that Dante could only see the brilliance of its light emanating from the top. Its rungs, filled with the spirits of thinkers and intellectuals, kept moving up and down. He also met St. Peter Damian who told him the story of his life and grumbled about corruption in the church.

Then it was on to the **Fixed Stars**. The Virgin Mary, Adam, St. John, St. Peter and St. James, along with a host of others, greeted Dante and tried to explain the glorious importance of and the connection between Heaven and the Garden of Eden.

Sphere **number nine** was the **Prime Mover**, where angels lived in nine rings surrounding a bright light.

Narrating the story of the creation of the world, Beatrice led him up to **Empyrean**, where God resided. Filled with love and peace, it was the highest place in

WHO WROTE IT AND WHY

Dante Alighieri wrote *Divina Commedia* or *The Divine Comedy* between 1300 and 1314 CE. In a hundred cantos or verses (three books of thirty-three cantos each), Dante narrates in Italian what he imagines is the three-stage journey of a Christian soul after death. The journey takes place on Good Friday and lasts till Easter Sunday. With just a single introductory canto, *The Divine Comedy* – with 'Inferno', 'Purgatorio' and 'Paradiso' – is considered to be one of the greatest works of literature.

Born to an aristocratic family in 1265 CE in Florence, Italy, Dante Alighieri was a medieval Italian poet, philosopher and writer who soon came to be famously known as just Dante. In a period when most literary works were in Latin, he wrote in an Italian dialect, thereby popularizing the local language. Deeply involved in the politics of the time, he fell afoul of the political powers and was exiled from Florence along with his sons in 1302 CE, never to return. He died of malaria in Ravenna in 1321 CE, when he was just fifty-six. *The Divine Comedy* was written during this period of exile and 'Beatrice' – around whom the manuscript is built – was a Florentine noble woman of the time.

His other notable works: *A Vita Nuova* or 'The New Life' (1294 CE), a collection of prose and poetry about courtly love; *De Monarchia* or 'On Monarchy', an essay in Latin (c. 1313); and *Eclogues* – poems (1319–20 CE, published only in 1719 CE).

His Muses: Six of them, including Calliope, the Muse of Poetry; Apollo, the Sun God; and Urania, the Muse of Astronomy.

Heaven. Covered in heavenly light, Dante saw a beautiful huge rose whose petals were home to the souls of the true and faithful.

Beatrice, her work done, took her place there while another soul, St. Bernard, led Dante to **three circles** where he came face to face with the splendour of God and the grandeur of the **Holy Trinity**.

Realizing that he too was a part of God's eternal love, Dante finally concluded his epic journey.

Of the two original copies of The Divine Comedy *in the world, reportedly one is with the Asiatic Society of Mumbai. It is said that they refused to part with it when, in 1930, Mussolini, the fascist ruler of Italy from 1925 to 1945, offered the sum of one million pounds sterling for it.*

THE RAMAYANA

How would you feel if you heard your entire life's story sung to you?

King Rama of Ayodhya sat forward. He wasn't quite sure if he was hearing right. It sounded familiar. Very familiar indeed.

The two boys Maharishi Valmiki had produced before him were in the middle of a ballad that the rishi himself had written. These boys had, during Rama's great Ashwamedha sacrifice, not only tied up his wandering horse and not returned it, but had also defeated the armies sent to rescue the horse.

So, of course he had wanted to meet them and listen to what they had to say. They spoke:

> Once upon a time in the land of a great king where life and livelihood prospered for the common man, the king himself was a sad old man.
>
> He had no heirs to rule his kingdom but do not fear, said his sages, we shall organize a grand yagna, sire.

If you partake of the sweet *payesh* that is cooked and share it with your three wives, we assure you, you will be blessed with not one but many sons.

Soon, true to the sage's words and to everyone's joy, the king's wives produced four strapping babies.

While wives one and two had one boy each, the third had a pair of twins.

In time, the boys grew up to be great warriors.

The eldest, the heir to the throne, was so brave and fearless that he was even called upon to slay a fearsome demoness who terrorized the neighbourhood.

He killed the demoness effortlessly, and then lifting Lord Shiva's bow that was deemed impossible to lift, he won the hand of a princess who was the loveliest in the land.

Soon, the happy king decided to abdicate in favour of his eldest heir.

A grand coronation was planned.

However, the eldest heir's stepmother, Kaikeyi, on the advice of her conniving maid, reminded the king of the two boons he had promised her long ago.

Recalling to his mind the two boons bestowed on her when she had once saved his life during a battle, the queen now said, 'Make my son, your second-born son, the king, and send the elder heir to the forest for fourteen years.'

A shocked and dismayed king tried to dissuade her, but the queen was adamant.

So, the eldest heir left the palace to go live in the forests.

Along with him went his devoted wife and one of his younger brothers as well.

Heartbroken, the king died soon after.

The second-born son, unhappy and angry at his mother's demand, begged his elder brother to come home and reign as king.

'But it was our father's wish,' insisted the eldest heir, refusing to do so.

So, the second-born son placed his eldest brother's sandals on the throne and swore to rule on his brother's behalf till he returned.

Meanwhile, the banished prince, his brother and wife wandered from forest to forest.

Until one day, a demon princess came upon them, and happened to fall in love with the handsome brothers.

She wanted to marry one of them.

They laughed at her.

Angry with their mocking, she attempted to attack the wife.

So, the brother, to protect his sister-in-law, brutally cut off the demon princess's nose and ears.

Bleeding and screeching in pain, she fled to her brother who was a powerful demon king.

To avenge his sister's humiliation, he sent the two brothers on a wild goose chase after a golden deer, which was actually a demon in disguise.

He then abducted the eldest heir's wife and carried her away in his *vimana* or airborne palanquin.

Searching for her frantically, the brothers stumbled upon a great bird who, with his dying breath, told them of the abduction and his battle with the demon king, up in the sky.

Finding some jewels that the abducted princess had flung out of the flying chariot, and seeing the sad plight of the prince, some *vanara* warriors came forward to help find her.

They searched far and wide till one of them, the son of the wind god – who was the *vanara* god himself – spotted her, sad and moping, in a garden guarded by demons on an island across the oceans.

He showed her a ring belonging to her husband and asked her to go back with him. 'Oh, I will wait for my husband to come fetch me,' she cried.

The demons spied him and set his tail on fire.

So, he, with great glee, hopped and skipped all around the kingdom, burning everything in his path.

Then, swinging his way back to the prince, he told him where he had found the love of his life.

Soon, with a formidable army of men, *vanaras* and other animals, this prince set out to rescue his princess.

He built a causeway across the sea and went forth to fight the wicked ten-headed demon king.

Shooting down all his ten evil head and destroying his demon army, the prince rescued his dear wife and placed the demon king's virtuous brother on the throne.

After his wife walked unscathed through fire to prove her purity, the three then joyously departed for home.

Their fourteen years of exile coming to an end and now the prince could be enthroned as he deserved. The new king ruled wisely and justly.

Then one day, he overheard a washerman condemn the queen for having lived in another man's land.

The good king now had to be seen to be doing the right thing.

So, he sadly bade his brother take his lovely innocent queen and leave her in the jungle once more.

The poor helpless queen, now expecting a child, found her way to a great rishi's ashram where...

●●●

'Stop,' said King Rama putting out his hand to interrupt the recital.

'How do you know all this? Who are you?' he asked the boys in shocked amazement.

For at that point, King Rama realized that the old king was perhaps his father Dasharatha.

The three wives were his mother Kaushalya, and stepmothers Kaikeyi and Sumitra.

The four sons could only be himself, with Bharata, Lakshmana and Shatrughna.

The boon-demanding stepmother had to be Kaikeyi while the jealous maid was Manthara.

Who else had been banished for fourteen years other than he himself, with his wife Sita and his younger brother Lakshmana?

Wasn't it the demon princess Surpanakha's nose that Lakshmana had cut off and wasn't she Lanka's demon king Ravana's sister?

While Lakshmana and he were fooled into searching for a golden deer, Ravana had indeed abducted Sita. So, the great dying bird who warned them had to be Jatayu.

Wasn't it also Hanuman's tail that had burned down Ravana's Lanka?

Then, building a causeway through the seas with Sugriva the *vanara* king's army, headed by Hanuman, hadn't they indeed rescued Sita?

Hadn't he, after killing the ten-headed Ravana, placed Ravana's brother Vibhishana on the throne, to finally return home?

So, now as an astonished Rama looked questioningly at the boys, Sage Valmiki stepped forward.

'These are your twin sons Lava and Kusha, O Rama,' he said. 'I told them your story.'

'My two sons?' Rama asked in wonderment. 'But where is Sita?'

Valmiki then brought her forward. 'Sita has been living in my ashram all these years,' he said.

Unable to contain his happiness, Rama said, 'Come back to me, O Sita. I have missed you. Go through another *agnipariksha* to prove your purity and return to me.'

WHO WROTE IT AND WHY

Maharishi Valmiki wrote the epic in 24,000 Sanskrit stanzas of seven *kandas* or books around 500–100 BCE to narrate the Ramayana (the 'Journey of Rama'), in which the protagonist Rama slays Ravana the demon king. It depicts the victory of good over evil.

Maharishi Valmiki is one of India's most celebrated Sanskrit authors. Born to a Brahmin family, he was a notorious waster, first known as Agni Sharma and then as Ratnakar – a highway robber – before he became a revered ascetic and a literary genius. A meeting with the sage Narada made him reflect on his follies and taught him the right way to live. It was then that Lord Brahma himself apparently told him to write the Ramayana since he was in fact witness to the life of Rama and Sita.

His other notable works: The first *shloka* or verse ever composed in Sanskrit literature is said to be by Valmiki – it was on the death of a bird in love shot down by a hunter. Thus, he is considered to be the *adi kavi* or the 'first poet' of Sanskrit literature.

Replied Sita with great love in her eyes, 'No, Rama. I am done.'

She then called upon her mother, Bhoomi Devi or Earth. 'If I am indeed pure, please take me back, Ma,' she cried.

The great earth split open at once and Sita disappeared into its cracks forever.

Soon after, a forlorn Lord Rama divided the kingdom between his sons and his nephews, and walked into River Sarayu, as did his brother Lakshmana.

Thus ends the epic Ramayana, which begins with a description of the city of Ayodhya and the gods waking Lord Vishnu from a deep cosmic sleep.

They urge him to go to Earth to rid the world of the omnipotent demon Ravana who, thanks to Brahma's boon, could only be defeated by a man and not by any spirit, demon or God.

So, Vishnu descended to Earth as a man, as Rama, the son of Dasharatha, and married Sita, to set events in motion.

Ratnakar turned over a new leaf and became a great Maharishi by sitting in meditation for so long that a 'valmiki', *meaning 'anthill', grew around him, hence the name.*

THE NIBELUNGENLIED

Wreak vengeance Kriemhild did, for the dastardly slaying of her beloved Siegfried, only to pay a terrible price...

'If you dreamed of a falcon being torn apart by eagles, your future husband will meet a violent death,' predicted her mother.

'I will not marry then,' declared beautiful Kriemhild.

However, marry she did, a brave prince known for his valour and courage.

Having won the enormous wealth of the Nibelungen clan from two brothers, called Nibelung and Schilbung, by dint of his sheer strength, and famed for it, Siegfried of Xanten landed up at Worms in Burgundy to seek fair Kriemhild's hand.

'You shall certainly marry her, sir,' said her brother, King Gunther of Burgundy, 'but only after you support me in defeating the Saxons who are even now threatening us, and then help me marry the proud warrior queen Brunhild of Iceland.'

'Why, what is the problem?' asked a mystified Siegfried.

'Brunhild insists she will only marry someone who outperforms her in throwing a spear, tossing a boulder and the length of her leap, or it's off with his head,' he said. 'Since I can do none of these things as ably as she can, and many have already lost their heads trying, I look towards you, Siegfried, to help me keep my head.'

Armed with a cloak that made him invisible whenever required and having bathed in the blood of a dragon he had slain, which made him invulnerable to attacks, brave Siegfried agreed.

So off to Iceland they went, to win the hand of the indomitable Brunhild for Gunther. The latter went as the king he was, with Siegfried pretending to be one of his subordinates.

Siegfried then put on his cloak of invisibility and, unknown to Brunhild, helped Gunther throw not only the javelin but the boulder too to a place far beyond where the eye could see.

He also carried Gunther along to leap a length that took Brunhild by surprise.

Fooled, Brunhild agreed to marry Gunther.

Even so, on their wedding night, Brunhild, to show off her immense strength, tied up a hapless Gunther and hung him from the bedpost.

So, an invisible Siegfried came to his aid again, freed him and helped Gunther win over his wife. However,

Siegfried took away a girdle and a ring as a keepsake for Kriemhild.

Siegfried then wed his beloved Kriemhild and home to Xanten they happily went.

●●●

Many years went by.

Then Brunhild, one day, decided to invite Kriemhild and Siegfried to Burgundy for a visit.

They accepted and were welcomed warmly.

Brunhild and Kriemhild enjoyed each other's company for a while.

However, soon, an argument about who was senior took place and, in anger, Kriemhild unknowingly blurted out the whole truth. 'Siegfried is an equal, not a vassal. He has helped Gunther in more ways than one.'

To prove it, 'Here, Brunhild, is your girdle and ring,' she said.

Haughty Brunhild was devastated and humiliated.

She realized she had been fooled all along.

She felt she had been shamed by Siegfried.

'Siegfried is not to blame,' declared Gunther. 'He is innocent.'

Unfortunately, a deeply mortified Brunhild did not believe him. She now wanted revenge.

So, she persuaded Gunther's cousin Hagen von Tronje to avenge her.

'It is my duty to protect your honour – so, Siegfried shall die,' promised Hagen.

'No, no,' pleaded Gunther weakly, 'Siegfried is not at all to blame.'

While Gunther did nothing to stop him, Hagen conjured up a false threat to Gunther's kingdom.

He then sought brave Siegfried's help to avert the threat.

'Of course, I will help you,' said a trusting Siegfried, hastening to his brother-in-law's aid once again.

Hagen then managed to worm out Siegfried's weak spot in his body from an equally trusting Kriemhild. Marking it out with a cross, 'It's for his own protection,' he said.

Then during their campaign, when Siegfried bent down to drink from a river, Hagen struck him at that very spot.

Siegfried died, and Hagen and Gunther returned home to falsely proclaim, 'He died in battle.'

However, during his funeral when Hagen went past the body, Siegfried's blood started to run. It was a divine sign that told a grieving Kriemhild that Hagen was the killer.

Next, cunningly getting hold of Siegfried's vast Nibelungen treasure, Hagen threw it in the Rhine.

Siegfried and Kriemhild

Why did he do that? To prevent Kriemhild from getting it. With wealth comes power, and Hagen knew that well.

'I swear, Hagen, I shall not forget,' a devastated Kriemhild promised herself. 'My time will come, when I will avenge Siegfried's death and the treasure you have stolen.'

Years passed, and Kriemhild married King Etzel of Hungary, though in her heart she never stopped mourning Siegfried.

A child was born and Etzel invited Gunther to the baptism ceremony.

A wary Hagen accompanied him and when Kriemhild accused him of having murdered Siegfried, he openly admitted to it. 'I did,' he said. 'Here is his sword. I also hid his treasure.'

A fuming Kriemhild then began to plot her revenge.

Outside the palace, a fight broke out between the visitors and the hosts.

As the fighting spread indoors, Hagen cut off the head of Kriemhild's baby in anger.

A shocked Kriemhild told her brother, 'Give up Hagen, make him tell me where the treasure is, or prepare to die.'

When Gunther refused, another fierce battle took place.

'Burn down the hall,' she ordered her men ruthlessly, 'with all the Burgundian guests in it.'

Without further ado, Gunther was also thus killed.

WHO WROTE IT AND WHY

Nobody knows who wrote it, but the *Nibelungenlied* or 'Song of the Nibelungs' in German, with its 2,400 stanzas in thirty-nine cantos, seems to have been around in Germany since 1200 CE at least, after a thirteenth-century manuscript was rediscovered by a doctor, Jacob Hermann Obereit, in 1755. Now, thirty-seven popular versions of it have been discovered. Composed nearly 800 years ago by an unnamed poet, today, A.T. Hatto's translation transforms an old text into a story as readable and exciting as Homer's *Iliad*.

Then when Hagen still refused to tell her where he had hidden the treasure, Kriemhild mercilessly slayed him with Siegfried's sword.

Now another guest, old Hildebrand, aghast and unable to prevent Gunther's or Hagen's killings, jumped into the fray and before Kriemhild was able to react, struck and cut her to pieces with his sword.

Thus ended the epic saga of the lovely Kriemhild and the brave Siegfried.

The betrayal and murder of Siegfried, as well as Hagen's character, were part of Nazi propaganda before and during the World Wars, to highlight the heroic nature and sacrifice of the German army.

THE MAHABHARATA

When cousins turn against each other and family fights family, what can you expect...

King Parikshit of Hastinapur placed a dead snake around the neck of a meditating rishi. Outraged at the insult, the rishi's son cursed the king thus: 'How dare you disturb him! May you die of snakebite.'

So, Parikshit built himself a tower where no snakes could possibly enter. However, Takshaka, the king of the snakes, slyly turned himself into a bug, hid himself in a fruit that was carried up to the tower, and then bit Parikshit to death.

Then, Parikshit's son Janmejaya vowed to kill every snake in the land. He organized a great 'Sarpa Satra' or snake yagna.

Among the many great kings and sages in attendance was Vaisampayana. He was Maharishi Vyasa's disciple.

During the yagna, as snakes from every nook and cranny found themselves helplessly drawn to the ceremonial fire to perish there, Janmejaya asked

Vaisampayana, 'Oh, respected disciple of my great-great-great-grandfather Vyasa! Could you tell me a bit about my venerable ancestors, how they lived and how they died?'

'Yes, indeed,' replied Vaisampayana. 'I will tell you what was narrated to me by the great Vyasa himself and written down by Lord Ganesha. Initially called "Jaya", it was all about the *mahayudh* or great war fought between his great-grandsons – the Kauravas and the Pandavas. It placed your Pandava great-granduncle Yudhishthira on the throne of Hastinapur but not before it had wiped out more than three generations of your family and friends.'

As Janmejaya nodded eagerly, Vaisampayana continued to speak:

Long ago, born to Hastinapur's King Shantanu and Ganga was a son Devavrata who became the heir to the throne. Unfortunately, Ganga left Shantanu and he later fell in love with a fisherwoman called Satyavati and wanted to marry her. However, Satyavati's father said, 'No marriage unless you promise to make your sons with Satyavati your heirs instead of Devavrata.' Shantanu refused to do so.

On seeing his father moping around the palace, Devavrata met Satyavati's father and promised to step aside for his future stepbrothers. 'I will not marry ever,' he promised, 'or have any children, I swear.' Thereafter, he was known to all as Bhishma (for he had taken this *bhishma* or 'terrible' oath).

Shantanu and Satyavati married and had two sons. When Shantanu died, the elder one became king, but he soon died in a skirmish. He was childless, so the younger son Vichitravirya was enthroned.

'We need heirs to the throne,' said Satyavati one day. 'Bhishma, find Vichitravirya a wife.'

So, Bhishma got a few princesses of a nearby kingdom to wed Vichitravirya. Though two of them became his wives, Vichitravirya too died childless.

Satyavati now begged Bhishma to marry. 'No,' he said. 'I will not break my vow.'

Unknown to everyone, Satyavati had another son by Sage Parashar long before her marriage to Shantanu. He was Vyasa and he was well on his way to becoming a great rishi. On Satyavati's request, he and Vichitravirya's widows decided to help the family line continue.

Their firstborn was Dhritrashtra, but he was born blind. The second was Pandu and he was born anaemic while the third born to a maid who had pretended to be one of the wives, was Vidur.

Now, Dhritrashtra, being blind, couldn't be king. Nor (in those times) could Vidur, born of a maid. Hence, Pandu became the king.

He was a good and able king, but he soon took himself off to the forests with his wives Kunti and Madri, leaving Dhritrashtra to rule with Bhishma's help.

Soon after, Pandu and Madri died.

Kunti, to the dismay of Dhritrashtra and his hundred sons, arrived in Hastinapur with her five sons – Yudhishthira, Bhima, Arjuna, Nakula and Sahadeva.

Kunti now wanted them to be brought up as heirs to the throne.

So, they too joined Dhritrashtra's boys, the Kauravas, at Dronacharya's *gurukul* and soon began to excel in every field.

There was no better archer than Arjuna in the land and no better wielder of the mace than Bhima.

Now, Yudhishthira, being older than Dhritrashtra's eldest son Duryodhana, was deemed to inherit Dhritrashtra's throne as well.

This displeased Duryodhana who believed and declared, 'I am my father's direct heir.'

Thus began the hostilities between the cousins.

Duryodhana began to do all he could to get rid of his cousins.

He even set fire to their palace, forcing them to take refuge in the forests.

Finally, Bhishma divided the kingdom between the Pandavas and the Kauravas.

Hastinapur remained under Duryodhana's rule while Indraprastha became the stronghold of the five Pandava brothers.

Indraprastha prospered and Yudhishthira became very popular.

Duryodhana was not happy.

So, he tried to insult his five cousins at every opportunity he found.

He also humiliated their common wife Draupadi time and again.

He then engaged and beat them in a game of dice not once but twice.

And finally, he had them exiled for thirteen years.

After that period had passed, when they returned, 'Not even a needlepoint of land, will I give you, Pandavas,' he proclaimed.

Though everyone, including Krishna, who was the Pandavas' cousin, told him that righteousness or dharma was with the Pandavas, Duryodhana refused to listen to reason.

So, war broke out between the Kaurava and Pandava cousins and their allies.

It was a horrendous war fought in Kurukshetra and it raged on for eighteen terrible days.

As many as 21,870 chariots, 21,870 elephants, 65,610 horses, 109,350 foot soldiers and numerous celestial weapons were used.

The blind King Dhritrashtra followed the war through his charioteer Sanjaya's eyes, even as it was being fought.

A war had never been seen on such a scale before. It was the Mahabharata war.

When it all ended, the Pandavas had won but lost almost everyone they held dear.

Duryodhana and all of the Kauravas too, except their teacher Dronacharya's son Ashwatthama, were killed. So also the grand old man Bhishma, and Dronacharya, their guru.

It was a terrible price to pay, but dharma or righteousness had won.

Yudhishthira, with his brothers, ruled for the next thirty-six years till they ascended to Heaven.

However, before they did, Yudhishthira placed Arjuna's young grandson Parikshit on the throne.

Parikshit had been in his mother Uttara's womb when his father Abhimanyu, Arjuna's son, was killed in the war.

'And you, Janmejaya, are his son,' Vaisampayana said.

WHO WROTE IT AND WHY

Maharishi Vyasa is said to have dictated the Mahabharata to Lord Ganesha at the insistence of Lord Brahma. Ganesha wrote it down in eighteen *parva*s or books compiled over a period between the third century BCE and the third century CE. With 100,000 verses, it is the world's longest epic. Embedded in it is Hinduism's holy text of 700 verses, the Bhagavad Gita. It is Lord Krishna's advice to Arjuna during the war.

Maharishi Vyasa, whose name means 'arranger' or 'compiler', is among the greatly revered sages of Hinduism, who compiled important religious texts that are followed to this day. Considered to be one of the 'Chiranjeevis' or immortals who remain alive on Earth eternally, Vyasa was the grandfather of the five Pandavas and the 100 Kauravas who fought the great Mahabharata war.

His other notable works: *The Vedas*: a large body of compiled religious texts constituting the oldest scriptures of Hinduism; *The Puranas*: sacred Sanskrit ancient texts covering myths, legends and other traditional lores; and *The Brahma Sutras*: Sanskrit texts that summarize Hindu philosophical ideas about the universe and human existence.

As a bemused Janmejaya nodded thoughtfully, Vaisampayana concluded, 'This then is the story of your ancestors and the terrible Mahabharata war they fought.'

And later, Sage Ugrasrava narrated this tale to some ascetics in the Naimisaranya forest, and they retold it to others, and so it went on...and that's how it became and continues to be the epic it is today.

The cave, Vyasa/Ganesha Gufa, where the Mahabharata was believed to have been written, exists in Uttarakhand even today. The fossilized rock roof resembles piles of palm-leaf manuscripts stacked on top of each other.

SILAPPADIKARAM

There was a terrible miscarriage of justice, and a city burns down...

The villagers watched the ethereal sight in awe.

A brilliant light spiralled up towards the sky from the hilltop yonder.

A grand chariot bathed in an equally bright beam appeared and swiftly escorted the light away into the Heavens.

'It's the chariot of Indra, the Lord of the Heavens... It has taken away Kannagi's spirit,' they murmured in disbelief and rushed to tell their king.

A bewildered Senguttavan, the Chera king, didn't quite know what to make of it till his poet Cattan stepped forward to tell him the story of Kannagi and her great love for Kovalan.

In the Chola town of Kaveripatnam, a marriage was arranged between Kannagi, the daughter of a rich sea trader, and Kovalan, the son of a wealthy merchant.

It was the grandest wedding the town had witnessed and the bride, the loveliest that anyone had seen.

However, the couple's happiness was not to last.

Kovalan, on one of his business trips, met a beautiful dancer called Madhavi and forsook Kannagi for her.

Kannagi, as expected, was heartbroken.

Soon there was trouble in Kovalan and Madhavi's paradise too.

They suspected each other of not loving the other enough, and when his money ran out, an apologetic Kovalan decided to return to Kannagi who was only too happy to forgive and take him back.

They set up home together once again and began to live happily as man and wife.

However, they too had no money.

So, they decide to move to the big city of Madurai in the neighbouring Pandyan kingdom to start life anew.

There, Kannagi gave Kovalan one of a pair of expensive golden anklets her mother had given her during their wedding and told him, 'Take this and pawn it. We can live off that money till you find a job.'

Kovalan dutifully went, and was not to be seen again.

A distraught Kannagi started to search for him until someone at the marketplace told her that Kovalan had indeed been seen at the pawnbroker's shop just that morning.

A passing herdswoman casually informed her, 'Oh, that man has been put to death on the orders of the king.'

'Why?' screamed a shocked Kannagi.

'For having stolen the queen's golden anklet, which he was then trying to pawn,' she was told.

'But that was *my* anklet,' she said angrily. 'It wasn't the queen's. Did the king not ask him how he came by the anklet before he put him to death?'

Then, finding Kovalan in a pool of blood, a grief-stricken Kannagi stormed into the palace.

Startled, everyone scattered in alarm.

The king, Nedunj Cheliyan I, himself stepped forward to ask, 'Who are you and what is it you want?'

'Oh, great Pandyan king, are you aware that the great Chola king of Poompahar, from where I come, executed his own son to ensure justice for a cow whose calf the prince's chariot wheel had run over and killed? Kovalan, the beloved son of a wealthy merchant, came to your city from that same town to earn a living. You, I hear, have wrongfully put him to death for trying to sell an anklet my mother gave me. As to who I am, I am the wife of that Kovalan and my name is Kannagi.'

'I did not wrongfully put anyone to death,' stated the king. 'The queen had lost her anklet and the pawnbroker said it was the same anklet. I believed him. The punishment for thieving is death.'

The king had indeed trusted the pawnbroker and so, without verifying the truth, had immediately ordered Kovalan's execution.

He was not to know that it was the pawnbroker who had stolen the queen's anklet and shifted the blame on Kovalan, a stranger in town.

'Then let me prove it to you,' Kannagi said and, asking for the anklet, broke it open right there. Out rolled emeralds and rubies.

The whole court gasped in shock. The king was absolutely stunned. So was the queen.

It was the tradition for royalty to fill their anklets only with pearls, not emeralds or rubies.

'Do you need any more proof, O King?' asked Kannagi in rage. 'Can you bring my husband back to life for me now?'

At this terrible miscarriage of justice, King Nedunj Cheliyan I, who was actually a very just and honourable man, died of instant shock and regret, as did his queen.

Kannagi's rage and grief was, however, so intense that she tore off one of her breasts and threw it across the city.

It burst into flames and Madurai began to burn.

The people, elephants, horses, charioteers and soldiers, all fled from the terrible fire.

However, before it could be destroyed completely, the goddess of the city appeared and calmed Kannagi down. 'You will join the husband you love so much in fourteen days,' she promised.

And that was how Kannagi was escorted by Lord Indra himself into Heaven.

'Is that right?' asked the Chera king, Senguttavan, as Cattan concluded the story of Kannagi. 'Then she must indeed be a goddess and should be honoured as such.'

Senguttavan decided to travel all the way up to the Himalayas in the north to get a special stone to carve her image on it.

WHO WROTE IT AND WHY

Ilango Adikal, a Jain monk and the younger brother of the Chera king, Senguttavan, wrote *Silappadikaram* between the fifth and sixth centuries CE, in 5,730 Tamil verses across three books named after the capitals of the southern kingdoms of the Cholas (Puhar), the Pandyas (Madurai) and the Cheras (Vanchi) where the events took place. He immortalized the powerful love of Kannagi for Kovalan and turned her into a goddess worshipped by the Tamil people.

Not much, however, is known about Ilango's life. Legend has it that to prove wrong the prophesy of an astrologer who had predicted Ilango would succeed his father to the throne, Ilango left his royal life, renounced the world and became a Jain monk. Through *Silappadikaram*, he showcases not only Tamil culture and history but also the arts. It describes city and village scenes, nuances of dance and music, town architecture, religions, and strikingly dramatic scenes of love and tragic death. One of the great achievements of Tamil genius, the *Silappadikaram* is a detailed poetic witness to Tamil culture, its varied religions, and the blend of Greek, Arab and Tamil peoples.

On the way he fought a few wars with his northern counterparts, emerged victorious and returned after purifying the stone in the waters of the Ganga.

He then had Kannagi's figure engraved on it as 'Goddess Pattini' and installed it in a temple (now about fifteen kilometres from Thekkady in Idukki district in Kerala), where it is worshipped even today.

Silappadikaram *('The Tale of an Anklet') is perhaps the only epic in the world that is centred around a woman. It is also among the oldest epics in the world, with the original manuscript, written on palm leaves, still in existence.*

MANIMEKALAI

What happens when a beautiful dancer becomes a Buddhist nun...

The Chola capital of Puhar was awash with excitement.

His hands vigorously working the huge, scented temple drums, the town crier announced from atop a majestic elephant that lumbered along, 'For the next twenty-eight days, beautify our town. Throw out hatred, and spread love and good cheer so that our ancient city may live long. The rains are plentiful and our king is benevolent. Indra, the Lord of the Heavens, has agreed to stay a while with us.'

Indra's festival was thus all set to be celebrated with great gusto.

As music and song filled the air, Chitrapati sent word to her beautiful granddaughter Manimekalai to join the dancers.

'No,' said Manimekalai. 'I will not dance at the festival. Like my mother Madhavi, I have turned to religion now. That will henceforth be my life.'

Chitrapati's lovely daughter Madhavi had been a courtesan and a famous dancer when she had met Kovalan and had their daughter Manimekalai.

After Kovalan had left her to go back to his wife Kannagi, and he had been tragically and unjustly put to death for an anklet he hadn't stolen, Madhavi had then turned to religion for comfort.

She had become a Buddhist nun.

Now their daughter too wanted to follow in her footsteps but not as a dancer.

To escape her grandmother, Manimekalai visited a garden nearby with her friend Sudhamati. And what a wonderful garden it was! As she wandered among singing nightingales, dancing peacocks, parrots that drank from golden plates and monkeys that hopped about in joy, she bumped into a prince.

He was Prince Udayakumar, heir to the throne of the Cholas. Mesmerized by her beauty, he began to follow her around. Though a nun was what she wanted to be, Manimekalai was confused because she too found him attractive.

'Manimekalai isn't interested in men like you,' Sudhamati said to him while Manimekalai herself slipped into a marble pavilion to lose herself among some stunningly lovely statues, which made it difficult for the prince or anyone else to find her.

However, the besotted prince was not prepared to give up.

Just then, her namesake, the goddess of the oceans, Manimekalai appeared. 'Go to Chakravala-Kottam, the Buddhist Temple of Heaven, to avoid the prince,' she ordered Manimekalai, 'You will be safe there.'

Then, putting her in a trance, the goddess spirited her off through the air to the island of Manipallavam.

•••

Waking up all confused, Manimekalai was at first assailed by memories of her past lives, the people in them and the sufferings that she had had to go through to arrive at her present birth and life.

She also remembered the unjust punishment meted out to her father, Kovalan.

Racked by unhappy thoughts, she suddenly spotted the Buddha's bejewelled footprints, which were only visible to a fortunate few.

Filled suddenly with immense inner peace, she decided that it was not the prince but the Buddha she would henceforth follow.

The goddess now appeared again and taught Manimekalai three mantras.

'Chant mantra one and you can whizz through the air without wings,' she said.

'Mantra two will enable you to change into any form, human or otherwise; and with mantra three you will never go hungry.'

Manimekalai was delighted. 'Would I ever need anything else?' she wondered.

The goddess then accosted Prince Udayakumar and told him, 'Leave Manimekalai alone. She is not for you. Her path is towards the divine.'

She also told Sudhamati and Madhavi, 'Manimekalai is safe. Do not look for her anymore.'

Tivatilakai, another goddess, then appeared. 'It is the great Buddha's birthday. Go to the lake on the island. There you will find a magic bowl, *Amrutha Surabhi,* that comes up only on Buddha's birthday. It will always be full and can feed any number of people. It belonged to one shipwrecked Aputhiran who died on this island. It is yours now.'

She also directed her to go meet the famous sage Aravana Adigal to know more about Aputhiran's life and Buddha's dharma. The wise man told her:

> One Aputhiran, accused of being a cow thief, ran away from home and began begging in front of a temple in Madurai. The goddess was pleased with his devotion. So, during a famine, she gave him a magic bowl, which automatically replenished itself. Aputhiran was happy. He could now feed everyone around him. However,

there came a time when he didn't need to feed anyone as the famine got over. So, he sailed to Indonesia where people were starving. However, on the way he was shipwrecked and he died on the island of Manipallavam.

Explaining the Buddhist theory of rebirth, which he said was dependent on the good deeds done in previous births, Adigal told Manimekalai to do the same: feed the poor and the homeless with the magic bowl.

A delighted Manimekalai did as instructed.

In the process, she started a charitable Buddhist clinic, and persuaded the king to release all prisoners and convert the prison into a monastery.

She then began to travel across the country as a *bhikshuni* or an alms-receiving nun.

●●●

It wasn't long after that the lovesick prince, egged on by Manimekalai's grandmother, appeared on the scene again.

'Please come away with me,' he begged her, 'I love you.'

Unnerved, Manimekalai decided to use mantra two given to her by the goddess.

She transformed her appearance and took on the face of one of her married friends.

She hoped he would go away if he believed she was a married woman.

As a confused prince hesitated, the friend's husband came on the scene.

He saw the prince begging someone who looked like his wife to run away with him.

Not knowing it was actually Manimekalai, he angrily cut off the prince's head.

Manimekalai was shocked.

So was the husband when he realized that it wasn't his wife the prince was declaring his love to, after all.

The king was aghast. 'Arrest Manimekalai and imprison her,' he ordered, while an even more furious queen sent someone to execute her.

WHO WROTE IT AND WHY

Kulavanikan Seethalai Satanar, a grain merchant, wrote *Manimekalai* between the second and sixth centuries as a sequel to *Silappadikaram*, in Tamil. Through supernatural happenings, it vividly describes in 4,861 lines and 30 cantos, the flourishing Tamil culture and Buddhism of the time.

Satanar is credited with transcribing the teachings of Lord Buddha from Pali, the language that the Buddha preached in, to Tamil for the first time. He is considered to be an important Tamil poet of Sangam literature, the earliest known literature of south India, and his *Manimekalai* soon went on to acquire epic status and he, great acclaim as a Buddhist poet.

The goddess, however, magically whisked her away.

Sage Adigal now convinced the queen: 'The fault lies with your son, O Queen. Not Manimekalai. It was your son's wrong behaviour that led to his death.'

The queen reluctantly forgave her.

As Manimekalai prostrated before the sage, he told her to always follow the path of dharma.

Manimekalai then went to Manipallavam where she had a miraculous meeting with Aputhiran of the magic bowl. Both prostrated before the Buddha's bejewelled footprints that were visible only to them and then flew off to the city of Vanchi to visit the Kannagi temple.

The king too now wanted to turn to religion, but Manimekalai told him, 'Your duty, O King, lies with the people as your kingdom needs you.'

Manimekalai then flew through the sky to meet her mother, and the sage and other great holy men in various cities where she learned more about the Buddha's doctrines: how to avoid numerous rebirths, prevent suffering and achieve Nirvana.

As she went about, changing her form whenever necessary, feeding the poor and spreading the Buddha's teachings, her life soon became the stuff legends are made of.

Behavioural psychologists have found many instances relating to mental health conditions in characters featuring in Manimekalai.

THE FAERIE QUEENE

When the virtues of Holiness, Temperance, Chastity, Friendship, Justice and Courtesy overcome all odds to help build a better kingdom...

Una rode agitatedly into Queen Gloriana's court on a snow-white donkey, leading a woolly lamb. She made straight for the throne.

Following her was a dwarf with a horse piled with armour meant for a knight.

She then knelt before the queen. 'I need help, Your Highness,' she cried. 'Having killed all our brave warriors, a horrific dragon has imprisoned my parents.'

Dressed in an all-white gown and a black cloak, Una looked beautiful.

Impressed, Georgos, a peasant, stepped forward eagerly, saying, 'Please let me go to their aid, Your Highness.'

'But you are not a knight,' said Una doubtfully.

However, the queen nodded her assent, and the moment he donned the knight's armour, Georgos turned into a noble knight and Gloriana named him the Knight of the Red Cross.

He now personified the virtue of Holiness and away he went to slay lovely Una's dragon.

This was how it was in imaginary Faerie Queene Gloriana's mythical court in Faerie Land.

Every knight there represented a desirable virtue. He or she then went on a mission to spread that virtue across the land for the queen.

From one adventure to another, they went to defeat the spread of vice or corruption caused by evil or unvirtuous people.

So, **Sir George** (Georgos) of the Red Cross, who embodied Holiness, fought to free Una's parents, who stood for Truth, from the dragon. Alongside, he also handled the monsters of Heresy and Error; the wizard Archimago, who symbolized Hypocrisy; and the evil Duessa personifying Falsehood.

So did the other knights who also went on similar adventures and missions.

They went on quests no different from George who was to later become the famous Saint George.

So, shall we meet some of these knights and see what they got up to?

- **Sir Guyon:** Personifying the virtue of Temperance or Moderation, he rode forth to bump into Arthur, a prince who was in love with Gloriana.

While Arthur narrated to him the glorious history of his country, Sir Guyon's constant companion, embodying Prudence and attired in black, egged him on to performing one heroic deed after another.

Teaching moderation to whomever they met, they headed for the enchantress Acrasia's Bower of Bliss.

Since she enticed young men to live a life of pleasure, Sir Guyon overcame strange beasts and monsters to destroy the Bower and free the young men.

He also met up with George and Una. Sir Guyon was one of Gloriana's favourite knights.

- Next was **Britomart**, who embodied the virtue of Chastity. Told by the wizard Merlin that it was her destiny to fall in love with another knight, Artegal, off she went to find him.

On the way, Britomart met Sir Scudamore who was looking for his bride Amoret, who had on their wedding day been captured by the evil wizard Busirane – who was now forcing her to marry him instead.

Britomart, who always longed to be a boy and so excelled in all the manly sports that the knights indulged in, easily rescued Amoret from Busirane, then was able to win a joust with Guyon and even tend to an injured George whom she met with Arthur.

- **Cambell** and **Triamond were** Gloriana's two other knights in shining armour.

Prince Arthur, the Knight of the Red Cross and Una

They symbolized the virtue of true Friendship. While they entered a tournament and showed great loyalty to each other, Britomart, another active participant in the tournament, unknowingly unseated and defeated Artegal, the man she was seeking.

Believing her to be a man and calling her to account for escorting Amoret about, both Scudamore and Artegal, who had been searching for Amoret, suddenly realized Britomart was a woman.

They apologized to Britomart, and Artegal, amazed at her talent, asked her to marry him. Scudamore, happy to have found his bride unharmed thanks to Britomart, was also now reunited with Amoret.

- **Sir Artegal**, who represented the virtue of Justice was next.

His mission was to rescue Princess Irena of Ireland from the giant Grantorto.

With Tallus, the defender of justice, Artegal killed the giant but not before having a few more adventures.

He, however, needed Britomart to rescue him from the Amazon queen Radigund, who had imprisoned him.

Arthur, whom everyone kept bumping into, and Artegal had other adventures too, when they helped free Queen Belge and her kingdom from the tyranny of the monster Geryoneo.

- Finally, there was **Calidore**, a knight who stood for the virtue of Courtesy.

WHO WROTE IT AND WHY

Sir Edmund Spenser, a famous English poet, wrote The Faerie Queene during 1590–96 CE to create a great national classic for England on the lines of other European epic poems. At over 36,000 lines and over 4,000 Spenserian stanzas – a verse form invented by him – *The Faerie Queene* is one of the longest poems in the English language.

Sir Edmund, long considered one of the world's greatest poets, was born in London in 1552 CE. He studied at the Merchant Taylor's School in Cambridge and completed his master's in 1576 CE. He served the English government for many years as a secretary to the Lord-Deputy of Ireland. After his first wife died, he married Elizabeth Boyle and addressed his popular sonnets (fourteen-line poems) to her. In 1589 CE, he returned to London to publish the first three of the six books of *The Faerie Queene*. Spenser died in 1599 CE when he was forty-six, leaving the *Faerie Queene* incomplete. A devout Christian and an ardent admirer of Queen Elizabeth I, he was buried in Westminster Abbey, London.

His other notable works: *The Shepheardes Calender* (1579 CE), a poem in twelve parts, each part dedicated to a particular month of the year; *Amoretti* (1595 CE), meaning 'Little Loves', a group of sonnets; and *Epithalamion* (1595 CE), a poem dedicated to his second wife, Elizabeth Boyle.

On a mission to capture the Blatant Beast, a loud monster representing Slander or False Statement, Calidore overcame many a deadly challenge in his quest. He met the knight Calepine and his lady Serena, who had been bitten by the Blatant Beast.

Calidore fell in love with the lovely shepherdess Pastorella and was determined to woo her.

Calidore managed to deliver the beast to Gloriana, but sadly it escaped to go about spreading its slanderous venom again.

Six virtuous knights representing six virtues and the adventures that befall them are contained in six long books that form the *Faerie Queene*.

Originally, there were to be twelve books of fantasy-filled adventures that happened to each of Gloriana's twelve knights, not just six, with each knight highlighting a virtue that would overcome a human failing. However, it remained incomplete due to the author's death.

The seventh, unfinished epitome was reckoned to be the adventures of Arthur, who represented the virtue of Magnificence.

The author believed that such virtues must be cultivated and imbibed by every citizen.

The Faerie Queene *is an allegory, a piece of writing with hidden meanings. Gloriana was based on Queen Elizabeth I who ruled England from 1558 to 1603 CE. Faerie Land was England, and all the knights and damsels were based on actual men and women of the court, who were easily identifiable.*

THE SHAHNAMEH

Persia's great legends Rustom and Sohrab and the adventures of their ilk are contained in the 'Book of Kings'...

'Ferdowsi,' said Sultan Mahmud of Ghazni, 'write about Persia, her great kings and her glorious history. I will pay you 1,000 gold coins for every couplet you write.'

'Oh, great Sultan, do not pay me in instalments,' replied Ferdowsi. 'Pay me when I am done. A lump sum in gold will help me to build an embankment across a river that floods and drowns my village every year.'

'Done,' said the Sultan, and in the summer of 977 CE, Persia's greatest gift to literature, Abul-Qasem Ferdowsi of Tus began his magnum opus that was to outlive the very empire he wrote about and is still read more than 1,000 years later.

He called it the *Shahnameh* or the 'Book of Kings'.

Combining myth, legend and history, he wrote about the creation of the world, and the genesis of Persia.

Next, he described the exploits of about fifty of her legendary (but perhaps mythical) heroes, known for their bravery and valour.

He then topped it off with the mind-blowing, and sometimes tragic, adventures of actual kings who ruled right up to the seventh century.

He wrote about:

- Shah Keyumars, the first king of Persia, who battled Ahriman the Devil.
- The good king Jamshid of Persia who fell from divine grace as he grew too arrogant and conceited for anybody's liking. Believing himself to be God, he wanted an elevated throne perched above the world.
- Evil Zohak of Arabia, the serpent king with two black man-eating serpents that darted out of his shoulders. Advised by the devil, he murdered his father, the noble king Mirtas, and then overthrew Jamshid of Persia and established a 1,000-year-long tyranny. So hated by his people was Zohak that they buried him alive, to and placed Jamshid's son Feridoun on the throne.
- The glorious reign of the wise king Feridoun. Happiness and peace reigned in Persia for 500 years. Feridoun divided his kingdom among his three sons. Unhappily, he saw the two eldest kill the youngest and then happily witnessed wise Minuchir, the

سنان دار نیزه بدو نیم گشت
چو رستم برادر بر انگونه یافت

Rustom kills his Turanian enemy with his lance

grandchild of the youngest, take back the throne, avenge his grandfather's murder and regain the family's past glory.

- The birth of Zal. His shock of white hair so upset his father Sam that he abandoned him to perish at the foot of the Alborz Mountain, which was made of jewels. Zal was saved and brought up by a bird of God, the red-and-gold-feathered eagle Simurgh. Sam, however, soon realizing his mistake, ferreted Zal out and took him home. With the valorous strength of a thousand great warriors and Simurgh's unstinting help, Zal became one of Persia's everlasting heroes.
- Zal and Rudabeh. How they fell deeply in love and to whom a legendary son, Rustom, was born.
- The miraculous birth of Rustom, the strongest of strong men who, even as a little boy, could with just one arm stop a rampaging white elephant, and – like his father Zal – became the bravest of brave warriors that Persia had ever seen.
- The adventures of red-haired Rustom. With his panther-skin cloak, ox-headed staff and leopard-skin saddle, Rustom underwent seven dangerous trials and more. On his devoted horse Raksh, he battled devils, and unimaginably ferocious lions and dragons, even while aiding other kings, during his remarkable 300-year rule.

- King Key Kavus, the often unfair ruler of Persia and his continuous feud with King Afrasiyab of Turan.
- The birth of Sohrab, son of Rustom, born to the lovely Tahmineh of Turan. He became a champion as brave as the father who was unknown to him.
- Rustom and Sohrab, father and son. Not knowing each other, they fought a war, only for Rustom to unknowingly kill Sohrab, and have him die in Rustom's grief-stricken embrace.
- The good prince Siyavash, son of Key Kavus. Accused of a crime he never committed against his stepmother, he comes unscathed through hell and fire, only to be unjustly killed.
- Kai Khasrau, son of Siyavash, who possessed the Cup of Divinity that could look into the future.
- Heroic Isfendiyar, son of Gushtasp, and his seven trials, similar to Rustom's – and how Isfendiyar died tragically at Rustom's hands.
- The death of brave Rustom. A severely wounded Rustom valiantly battled his treacherous stepbrother Shoghad, only to finally succumb to his injuries, along with his faithful steed Raksh.
- The struggle and fall of the seventh-century Sassanian dynasty to the invading forces of the Arabs.
- The arrival of Islam and the Caliphate in Persia.

WHO WROTE IT AND WHY

Abul-Qasem Ferdowsi composed *The Shahnameh* on the order of Sultan Mahmud of Ghazni, in 60,000 rhyming couplets in Persian. Covering 990 chapters through four generations of rulers across three parts, *The Shahnameh* narrates Persia's celebrated history. Initially performed and passed on by word of mouth by Naqqalis or travelling storytellers, the sixty-two glorious stories of *The Shahnameh* even now mesmerize audiences the world over.

Acknowledged as one of Persia's greatest poets, Abul-Qasem Ferdowsi was born to a family of Persian landowners on the outskirts of the ancient city of Tus in the Khorasan province of Iran. Since the Islamic conquests of the seventh century had a strong cultural impact on Iran, Ferdowsi probably felt the need to preserve the pre-Islamic history and myths of the ancient Persian peoples. Though not too much is known about his personal life, an elegy written and included in *The Shahnameh* indicates his immense sorrow at the death of a 37-year-old son. Ferdowsi reportedly died sometime between 1019 and 1025 CE, during the rule of the Ghaznavids.

When Ferdowsi had finally finished his epic narration, the Sultan's middleman paid him his 60,000 coins, not in gold but in ordinary silver. An annoyed Ferdowsi felt cheated and gave it all away.

This act angered the Sultan who thought him ungrateful, so Ferdowsi had to flee the kingdom.

When the Sultan realized the truth and sent him the coins in gold, it was too late. A bitter and angry Ferdowsi had just died and the embankment across the river remained unbuilt till much later.

However, what came true was his forecast: 'As this famous book comes to an end, the country will be full of talk about me… I will not die after this, I will remain alive, as I have scattered the seeds of speech.'

It took Ferdowsi thirty-three years, from 977 CE to 1010 CE, to complete The Shahnameh.

THE LUSIADS

Determined the Portuguese were, to discover a sea route to India...

'The route to India is fraught with danger,' proclaimed a voice from among the crowd on the beach. 'Do not be reckless. Look for conquests nearer home. If you go chasing fame and fortune, you will lose your lives.'

However, Vasco da Gama ignored it and ordered his men to set sail.

On Mount Olympus in Greece, Jupiter, the king of the Roman gods, called for an urgent meeting of his divine council.

'Vasco da Gama, with his armada of ships is, even now as I speak, navigating the waters of unknown seas to bring great glory to Portugal,' he stated. 'He has set sail to discover the sea route to India.'

'India is mine,' argued Bacchus, the god of wine. 'Portugal shall not take it away.'

His support was for Asia and the Moors who were Muslims and populated most of Asia, while the others were rooting for the Christians in Europe, who wanted to spread their wings and take over.

'Why not?' asked Venus, the goddess of love. 'It is good news for us, isn't it?'

'I agree, Venus,' added Mars, 'after all, the Portuguese are Roman descendants too. Should we not support them?'

'Yes,' nodded Jupiter. 'I shall dispatch Mercury, the messenger god, at once to escort them safely.'

Bacchus kept quiet. He was nevertheless determined to see that Vasco da Gama failed in his quest.

So, when da Gama's ships reached Mozambique, their first port of call, Bacchus slyly incited the local people to attack them.

However, da Gama fired his guns, and they backed off, terrified. They even promised to have a guide escort the Portuguese fleet of four ships to Mombasa.

Bacchus got down to work again. They were now led astray by their guide and went not to Mombasa but into the hostile waters of Quiloa, where Bacchus was all set to have them killed.

Venus and Mars quickly stepped in and stopped them from entering the port.

The helpless guide, with no other option, turned away and steered them to Mombasa as earlier planned, where again Bacchus was plotting their death.

However, Venus and Mars again foiled his attempts.

Despite the difficulties stirred up by Bacchus, the two blocked the harbour and prevented the ships from entering Mombasa.

They then went running to Jupiter for help.

Once again, Jupiter sent Mercury to escort them out safely.

The ships sailed past Morocco, Madeira, the Canary Islands, Mauritania and the Congo. They spotted the stars of the Southern Cross and watched St. Elmo's spark of fire in awe, to finally reach the Cape of Good Hope.

There they were attacked not by mere storms but by the spirit of the Cape, a terrible, monstrous Titan-turned-rock called Adamastor, endowed with superpowers, who threatened them with even more frightful dangers.

Then, narrowly surviving several other nerve-wracking storms, the fleet managed to escape – though many died from scurvy and other illnesses on board – to finally drop anchor at Malinda.

At Malinda, the king welcomed them with great cordiality. He visited Vasco da Gama on his ship and da Gama regaled him with stories of brave Portuguese heroes and legends, of great discoveries and Portugal's glorious history.

Vasco da Gama also brought him up to speed about their journey so far.

Impressed with the greatness of Portugal, and in return for his hospitality on board, the king sent him off with an escort to get him to India.

Bacchus, however, was not done. Through Neptune, the god of the seas, he stirred up some terrible squalls, where the fleet was thrown around alarmingly by fierce, stormy waves.

Almost on the verge of death, a desperate Vasco da Gama sent up a prayer.

So, a second council of gods was held, and Jupiter sent Venus to Vasco da Gama's rescue yet again.

She calmed the waves, weakened the swirling storms, and saw them through to quieter waters.

●●●

As the beaches of Calicut in India finally rose out of the sea to meet them, they were spotted by Moncaide, a Muslim trader.

'Welcome, welcome,' he said but cautiously. 'Where do you come from?'

'From across the world – we have reached here after eleven months at sea,' replied Vasco da Gama excitedly. 'Do tell us about this new land, its people, its culture and traditions.'

So, Moncaide told them all about Calicut and took him to meet the great ruler, the Zamorin.

Impressed by the great carvings, the art and the architecture around him, Vasco da Gama, however, disapproved of the idols he saw in the temples. He believed he came from a superior country since he was a Christian but, 'I come in peace, Your Highness, to trade,' he said to the Zamorin.

So, a trade agreement was in the offing, but Bacchus played mischief again.

'They are Christian pirates who are out to cheat you,' he told the Muslim tradesmen and turned them against Vasco da Gama.

As a result, the moment Vasco da Gama went ashore with his wares, he was detained by the Zamorin's men.

When he was being taken away, da Gama's crew, worried for his life, fired shots, and in that confusion, da Gama managed to escape.

WHO WROTE IT AND WHY

Luis Vaz de Camoes composed *The Lusiads* in 1572 CE in ten cantos of 1,102 stanzas to highlight the glory and greatness of Portugal as a premier seafaring Christian European country. With large dollops of fantasy thrown in, *The Lusiads* – meaning 'Sons of Lusus (the founding father of the Portuguese) – is dedicated to King Sebastian of Portugal and is based on Vasco da Gama's actual journey via the Atlantic Ocean to discover India (in May 1498).

Born in Lisbon around 1524–25 CE, Luis Vaz de Camoes was one of Portugal's great poets. With connections to the rulers of Portugal and Spain, his family was part of the old aristocracy. Often compared to Shakespeare, Milton, Homer, Virgil and Dante, Camoes was well versed in the classics, though it is uncertain where he studied or attended university (it could have been at Coimbra in Portugal). Many references in his poems indicate that he not only lived in Morocco for a while but also travelled around for a few years. Apart from taking part in naval expeditions, he was possibly shipwrecked in the River Mekong (which flows down from the Tibetan plateau to the South China Sea in Asia) before he began writing his masterpiece in Macau. Camoes returned to Portugal in 1570, and *Os Lusiadas* or *The Lusiads* was published in Lisbon soon after. His importance is known by the fact that he was granted a royal pension. Camoes died in 1580.

His other notable works: *Auto El-Rei Seleuco, Disparates da Índia, Auto do Filodemo* and *Anfitrioes* (1587).

His Muse: Calliope, the Muse of Poetry

Back on board, he quickly turned his fleet around and left with whatever he had managed to trade. It wasn't much, but was still a lot more than he had come with.

To his relief, the Zamorin, magnanimously, let him go.

Chased by Muslim traders, as da Gama rapidly tried to steer himself away, Venus with her nymphs came to his rescue once again.

She helped them escape to the Isle of Love.

They spent a few days there relaxing and toasting the success of their discovery of a route to India.

Tethys, a Greek goddess, regaled them with the history of African and Indian explorations, and Magellan's trip around the world.

Then, predicting a great future for the Portuguese in India, the story of Vasco da Gama's epic journey to India as envisioned by the poet, came to an end.

Cameos actually went on a similar sea voyage to experience what Vasco da Gama and his sailors went through during 1497–98 CE. He went first to India, then on to Macau in China and returned to Lisbon by way of Africa.

THE EPIC OF KING GESAR

When the forces of evil run amok, God sends a saviour to the rescue...

'A Council of the Gods met in Heaven,' warbled the travelling bard, 'to discuss what was happening in the land of Tibet below.'

'Rescue we must the good people of Tibet,' said the Lord of Heaven, 'from those powerful marauding demons and wicked spirits who seek to destroy their lives.'

'Yes,' nodded the others. 'And so shall we a saviour to Earth send, to defeat those forces of evil?'

'Certainly,' they agreed, and so – though versions of the tale differ in the details – created through a magic potion, a godchild called Gesar.

And thus began the story of the great king Gesar...

Born on Earth, the divine Gesar turned out to be an ugly little baby. His mother belonged to the Ling kingdom.

His jealous uncle Trothung felt threatened by the little boy, who it had been prophesied, might overthrow him. So, he began to ill-treat and hound the mother and son.

He was not to know, though, that Gesar's divinity and supernatural powers would come to the young man's rescue every time.

And so, it was. Nothing he did could destroy Gesar.

However, unable to get rid of him but hoping to safeguard himself permanently, Trothung banished Gesar and his mother from his kingdom.

Growing up in the wilds, raised among the fierce animals of the forests and by the river, Gesar grew brave and strong.

With superhuman strength and magical powers, he roamed the jungles on his flying steed and was afraid of nothing.

Then, one day, when he was in his early teens, he ran a race.

He had heard that there was a horse race in his uncle's kingdom where the participants competed for the Ling throne.

So, along went young Gesar with his devoted horse and competed in the race of his life, to win not only the Ling throne but also the hand of the beautiful princess Brug-mo from a neighbouring kingdom.

He then, without much ado, threw out his uncle, proclaimed himself king and set about ruling his subjects wisely and well.

A painting depicting King Gesar of Ling

Using his divine powers whenever required, he went on long campaigns to defend, fortify and stabilize his kingdom.

He led his brave and loyal soldiers to overcome one demon after another and reconquer some eighteen and more fortresses.

After all, he was a half-god, wasn't he?

He also began to expand his territory. He then redistributed the enemies' wealth among the people of Ling.

Thus, quelling all rebellions and vanquishing all evil spirits and demons, he finally ushered in an era of peace and prosperity for the people of Greater Tibet (the Ladakh, Kargil, Baltistan and Gilgit of today).

However, hell was soon to break loose.

●●●

One night, when Gesar was away on a campaign, his beautiful bride was abducted.

The king of Hor, also known as the White-Tent King, coveted her for her beauty and wanted to make her his wife.

Now, the good king Gesar couldn't allow that, could he? He had to get his queen back.

So, the kingdoms of Ling and Hor went to war.

King Gesar was outranked and outflanked by the Hor army, and the Ling capital fell to the Hors.

WHO WROTE IT AND WHY

Nobody knows who composed *The Epic of King Gesar*, but it was probably done around 200–300 BCE. Though it was compiled only in the twelfth century by Buddhist monks, King Gesar's exploits soon filled not one but 120 volumes of more than one million verses and twenty million words divided into twenty-nine chapters – and still counting. This epic that begins with an invocation to Buddhism, has been added to right up to the twentieth century. Thus, King Gesar's story has easily become one of the longest continuing epics of the world with each imaginative retelling. Though the origins of this epic are lost in the mists of time, *The Epic of King Gesar* has about 180 different song and narration versions.

Even so, with great courage and fortitude, Gesar regrouped his soldiers and took the battle right into the Hor kingdom.

Riding his magic steed, he captured the Hor capital, killed the evil White-Tent King, and rescued his queen, but not before he had cleverly laid a trap to slay all his enemies who guarded around nine outlying defensive bridges, thus, reunifying all that land under him, as well.

His reputation as the ablest of able kings soon spread far and wide across Central Asia, from Mongolia to Tus.

Even the initially reluctant Buddhist monks began to extol his virtues.

'He is not only brave, but he is enlightened too,' they said.

'After all, within just three days of his birth, didn't he get rid of the rats that plagued our fields? Didn't he later even rescue his dear mother from Hell?' they exclaimed. 'The Lord of Heaven sent him to Earth to rescue us from our enemies from Hell.'

So strong is their faith in him that the Tibetans even today firmly believe that he has disappeared from their lives only momentarily, and would return from a divine place called Shambhala to rescue them once again when the need arises, or so says this epic.

It is a 'living' epic. The entire original oral epic is still to be found in handwritten books, and new episodes, revealed through divine vision or revelation to Buddhist monks or religious bards, are being continuously added. King Gesar's sword and saddle can be found displayed in the exhibition hall of the Labrang Monastery in Tibet.

THE ILIAD

The tale of a face that launched a thousand ships and brought many a nation to its knees...

It had been nine long years. Brave battles were being won and lost. Yet the war was not done. The Greeks were camped outside Troy, even as the Trojans relentlessly defended their city. Arrayed against each other were heroes legendary for their courage and bravery.

If the Greek camp had…

- Achilles, the greatest warrior in the world and leader of the Myrmidon contingent;
- Agamemnon, the Greek–Achaean commander-in-chief of the combined Greek armies;
- Menelaus, the brave but aggrieved King of Sparta, and Agamemnon's brother;
- Odysseus, Greek hero and the king of Ithaca;
- Aias the Great, second only to Achilles in bravery; and
- Patroclus, Achilles's closest friend and fearless warrior…

The Trojans had…

- Hector, Prince of Troy, and the greatest of all Trojan warriors;
- Priam, the aged king of Troy;
- Paris, the eldest son of Priam and a prime cause of the war; and
- Aeneas, the greatest of Trojan warriors after Hector.

Both the armies had Olympian gods on their sides too.

While Zeus the king of the gods tried to remain neutral, Poseidon (the god of the sea), Hera (the goddess of marriage) and Athena (the goddess of wisdom) rooted for the Greeks, with Apollo (the god of music and the Sun), Aphrodite (the goddess of love and beauty), and Ares (the god of war) actively helping the Trojans.

Thus, with divine help, the two sides were evenly poised and the Trojan War, as it came to be known, swung this way and that, with no outright winner.

As the war continued, 'Please return my daughter Chryseis to me,' pleaded her father to Agamemnon. Agamemnon who had taken Chryseis as a Trojan captive, however, refused to do so.

So Chryseis's father and Apollo's chief priest begged Apollo to intervene.

Apollo promptly brought down a plague on the Greek–Achaean army.

For nine full days, the plague spread wildly, taking lives by the dozen.

Until a desperate Achilles went to Agamemnon and told him to please return Chryseis to her father so that the dying would stop.

'All right, I shall,' agreed Agamemnon truculently, 'but I shall take the lovely Briseis, whom you have captured, instead.' Briseis was the wife of King Mynes of Lyrnessus, an ally of Troy.

Then, without so much as a nod from Achilles, he had Briseis shifted to his own camp.

Chryseis went home and the plague was called off.

However, Achilles was livid. He was a proud man, you see.

He hadn't wanted to part with Briseis.

Though she was a captured Trojan, she had been a great favourite of his.

He had also won her in battle, fair and square.

So, Achilles felt humiliated and insulted at Agamemnon's summary action.

Full of angry pride, he now refused to fight under Agamemnon's command any longer.

Instead, he called upon his mother Thetis, a sea nymph, to help the enemy, the Trojans, instead.

'Let Agamemnon realize how helpless he is without me by his side,' he said.

Thetis went to Zeus for help who, though apparently neutral, was unable to say no to her.

Slowly, the Trojans began to gain the upper hand.

As Agamemnon suffered loss after loss, a vengeful Achilles watched from the sidelines.

●●●

Reader, are you now wondering what this war was all about?

For that, we need to go back a few years.

In a series of flashbacks, we find out that it all started when Paris, Prince of Troy, with the help of the goddess Aphrodite, whisked the lovely Helen away from her husband, King Menelaus of Sparta.

Menelaus called on his Greek allies to help get Helen back and they set sail with a thousand ships to bring Helen home from Troy.

However, despite the Greek coalition's best efforts, it wasn't easy.

The powerful city of Troy was no pushover and defended herself fiercely.

As beautiful Helen watched her husband and his allies fight to rescue her, the war went on for nine weary years.

Then, to top it all, Achilles, the one person who could have won the war single-handedly for them, became aggrieved.

To be fair, at one point, King Menelaus did fight Paris, one-on-one.

He would have won too, but for Aphrodite who had swooped down to save Paris.

So now, as the Trojans began to slowly emerge as the victorious side, 'Please Achilles, come back and fight,' pleaded everyone.

Achilles, however, still furious with Agamemnon, refused to relent.

Being touchy, he preferred instead to angrily brood by the sea over the wrong done to him.

Unable to convince him, Patroclus, his very best friend, donned his armour. Then, pretending to be Achilles, he took the fight into the enemy camp.

A fearless Patroclus was killed by Hector, the beloved prince of the Trojans.

A shocked and grieving Achilles now put aside his anger against Agamemnon and rejoined the action.

Mad with rage, he was determined to avenge his dear friend's death.

In a special armour made for him, Achilles now went looking for Hector.

He also went on a killing spree as never was seen before, slaughtering as many Trojans as he could so that their bodies filled the nearby river. It even caused the river god to rise in outrage.

●●●

Finally, when he did find Hector, Achilles chased him around Troy's city walls at least three times before they faced off.

A mighty battle then took place.

And amidst shattered chariot wheels, flying horses, crushed limbs and broken necks, Achilles killed Hector. Heroic Hector, who was to Troy what Achilles was to the Greeks. A superhero who himself had singly taken on and killed no less than 30,000 Greek soldiers.

Achilles, however, was not satisfied with merely killing Hector.

He also wanted to insult the Trojans and their now dead hero.

So, he tied Hector's body to his chariot wheel and, raising clouds of dust behind him, dragged it all the way back to the Greek camp.

Then, for nine whole days, he hauled it around Patroclus's body as Patroclus's funeral rites took place and celebratory funeral games were played in the Greek camp.

The gods finally put a stop to it.

Then, in the dead of night, old king Priam of Troy went to Achilles. He asked for his son's body back.

Achilles now felt ashamed at his own unchivalrous behaviour. Contrite, he called a truce and then handed the body over for a proper funeral.

While the see-saw siege of Troy continued, the epic story of Achilles's fierce anger against Agamemnon

WHO WROTE IT AND WHY

Homer, a blind Greek poet in the eighth century (750) BCE, wrote *The Iliad* in twenty-four books of 15,693 lines in ancient Greek. *The Iliad*, sprung from the word 'Ilium' – another name for Troy – is among the most famous narrated epics of the world. It covers the action of a period of four days and two nights in the tenth year of the Trojan War. The warfare strategies described were so authentic that great warriors including Alexander the Great of Macedonia used it as a guide for their battles.

Considered one of the world's greatest poets, Homer is believed to have been born in the eighth or ninth century BCE in Iona, now in Turkey. So shrouded in mystery is his personal life that scholars use his works to interpret and understand him. For instance, he is presumed to be blind because of the description of a blind poet in *The Odyssey*, his other famous work, or it is believed that he left Cyme (in present-day Turkey) because the government there would not support him at public expense – a point mentioned in another work. He also appears to have influenced other famous poets, ranging from as early as Virgil (70 BCE) and Dante (1321 CE) to the eighteenth-century Alexander Pope, who all acknowledge his greatness in their works. Credited for introducing 'Homeric Greek' – a form of Greek language – to the world, he has through his epics established the Homeric tradition, now an integral part of European classical literature. Much of his works have been lost in time, but the ones that have survived – such as the Homeric epics – have had a tremendous global impact, inspiring many famous works of literature, music, art and film.

His other notable work: *The Odyssey* (ninth century BCE), a sequel to *The Iliad*.

His Muse: Calliope, the Muse of Poetry.

and his victory over Hector came to an end with Hector's funeral.

British kings are believed to be descendants of a Trojan, Prince Brutus, who not only escaped the fall of Troy but also founded the city of London. How far this is true is anybody's guess.

Interestingly, it has been estimated that reading at a speed of 300 words per minute, it would take seven hours and seven minutes to complete The Iliad.

THE ARGONAUTICA

In search of the Golden Fleece did Jason and the Argonauts go...

Phrixus was stunned. He had just overheard his stepmother Ino make arrangements to have him sacrificed to the gods to avert a famine. And his father, King Athamas of Iolcus, to Phrixus's utter shock, raised no objections.

'We must leave Thessaly,' said his sister Helle at once. 'Oh, how I wish Mother was alive.'

Just then, a golden-fleeced, winged ram appeared before them. 'Use this to escape,' commanded their mother's voice. 'And get away fast.'

Without much ado, in the darkness of the night, Phrixus and Helle clambered on to the ram and tried to get as far away as possible.

Sadly, however, as they flew over the oceans, Helle toppled over and drowned. That spot for evermore came to be known as the Straits of Hellespont.

Phrixus, on the other hand, travelled so far that he reached a place called Colchis, off the shores of the dangerous Black Sea, ruled over by King Aeetes who kindly offered him shelter.

Phrixus then sheared the divine Golden Fleece off the ram and hung it up safely in Aeetes's grove of Ares. He soon married Aeetes's daughter and settled down in Colchis.

The Golden Fleece signified great power and wealth. So, it was constantly guarded by a fiery dragon and a coiled serpent.

And that is where it stayed. Many years later, Pelias became the king of Iolcus in Thessaly, having usurped his brother Aeson's throne. Pelias ordered his young nephew Jason to bring back the Golden Fleece, if Jason ever wanted to be king. The Golden Fleece was still guarded by the fire-breathing dragon.

Unknown to Jason, it had been prophesied that he was a threat to Pelias. So, Pelias wanted him gone forever.

And that is where Jason's adventures began.

●●●

The route was fraught with danger and no one who had gone seeking it had come back alive.

Pelias knew that, and so did Jason.

However, that didn't deter Jason. Strong and able-bodied as he was, he decided to try his luck.

With help from Athena, the goddess of wisdom, he built himself a sturdy ship, the *Argo*.

Then with a band of around fifty men called the Argonauts, he set sail to recover the Golden Fleece from King Aeetes.

Their first stop was the island of Lemnos, where lived foul-smelling women who fed off men.

The queen of the island fell in love with Jason and told him, 'I want you to stay.'

Jason was tempted, but the others were not.

They managed to escape with their limbs intact to wash up on the shores of strange, unfriendly six-armed savages, only to get into a fight with a group called the Doliones, whose king Jason unknowingly killed.

Then, battling terrible stormy winds, they somehow reached River Cius where they found they had lost some of their young members to a few loving sea nymphs.

They nevertheless sailed on to arrive in the land of King Amycus and the Bebrycians.

Coerced by the locals to participate in duels, the depleted crew bravely did so. They won, only to be threatened and chased by them.

Forced to quickly make their escape, they stumbled upon an island with an old and blind seer, King Phineas, who had been punished by Zeus for leaking divine secrets.

As punishment, he was to be tormented by monstrous inhuman birds with human faces called Harpies, who would heinously defile his food to starve him.

Jason's men drove the Harpies away for good and poor old Phineas was thrilled.

So, he gratefully drew them a route to Colchis and warned them about the Symplegades, a pair of rocks that moved together whenever anything passed between them, to crush it.

'Send a dove through it first,' he said, 'then quickly follow before the rocks clash or you might get smashed in between.'

However, when they did so, the rocks brushed the dove's wings, and in their follow through, their ship's stern also scraped the rocks.

It was Athena again to their rescue. Into the Black Sea she guided them, as quickly as she could, before the shifting rocks crushed them.

Spotting Apollo whizzing along on the horizon, they offered up thanks to him for having got them this far, and steered themselves past the River Acheron.

There, at one of the entrances to Hades (Hell), they needed to appease ancient ghosts to be able to carry on.

Then, trying to avoid the waters of the Thermodon, the river of the aggressive Amazons, they were suddenly attacked by the savage birds of the war god Ares.

As they desperately fought them off, four sons of Phrixus along with the grandsons of Aeetes joined them too.

Soon, Zeus's huge eagle was seen flying overhead over the Caucasian Mountains where it fed daily on Prometheus's liver. Prometheus, the god of fire, was nailed to the rocks as punishment for disobeying Zeus.

To their good luck, the Argonauts suddenly found themselves tossed ashore on one of Colchis's seaward back-bays.

'How do we now get hold of the Golden Fleece?' they asked each other.

And to their aid once more came Athena and Hera, the queen of the gods, and the goddess of marriage, women and family.

Taking Aphrodite's help, they made Aeetes's daughter Medea fall madly in love with Jason.

'I will convince my father to give it to you,' she promised. However, her father wasn't persuaded.

Instead, he set Jason an impossible task, certain to have all the sailors die.

'Plough the land of Ares using fire-breathing bulls, then sow four acres of the land with the fiery dragon's teeth, and finally kill the armed men that will sprout out from its teeth,' commanded the king.

A lovesick Medea, whom Jason had promised to marry, came to his aid again. She gave him a magic balm.

Dabbing himself with some of it, he entered the dragon's lair.

Not only did the magic balm protect him from the fiery bulls but, much to the king's bewilderment, Jason was able to easily handle the bulls, the dragon's teeth and the stone soldiers that sprang up.

Disappointed, the king decided to get rid of Jason some other way.

However, Medea had other ideas.

She put the fire-breathing dragon and the coiled serpent to sleep with her magic spells, and enabled Jason to steal the Golden Fleece and make good his escape from Colchis with her.

A furious Aeetes, not to be outdone, sent armed ships to bring the Fleece and his daughter back.

A battle took place and Jason slayed them all, including Medea's brother, and set the *Argo* on course for Thessaly.

WHO WROTE IT AND WHY

Apollonius of Rhodes in Alexandria (Egypt) wrote *The Argonautica* in the late third century BCE in Homeric style. Across four books of about 6,000 lines, he hoped to record the famous deeds of ancient men and heroes.

Like many other poets of olden times, the life of Apollonius of Rhodes too is a mystery. The little we know comes from many different sources, some of which are conflicting. A Greek poet and grammarian, he is believed to have become a librarian in 260 BCE until he fell out of favour under a new king in 247 BCE. However, he was both creative and influential, and his writing style was a great model for other emerging Latin poets.

His Muses: Apollo, the Sun God, as well as Erato, the Muse of Lyric Poetry.

Jason and Medea then got married and even though Aeetes called off the chase when he came to know that, it still was no easy sail for them.

Avoiding the sorceress Circe and the three wicked Sirens who with their songs lured sailors to crash onto their rocks, the *Argo* was treacherously blown off course many a time.

Then, though certain death faced them, through a desert they walked for miles, carrying the *Argo* on their shoulders, to get to the open seas, which would finally lead them home. Further misfortune befell them when the cunning giant Talos of Crete tried to stop them.

They overcame him with some more of Medea's magic, only to be hit by a dark, treacherous fog.

Apollo came to their rescue now. He lit up a path through the fog to help them finally reach Iolcus, where they placed the Golden Fleece safely in Poseidon's grove in the Isthmus of Corinth.

And thus successfully did end Jason's epic journey to recover the Golden Fleece.

With a band of twenty oarsmen in a 54-foot-long Bronze Age replica of the Argo, *India-born British explorer Tim Severin sailed Jason's route of 2,400 kilometres in 1984.*

THE KALEVALA

Land of Heroes, where battles were won with songs instead of swords, knowledge instead of blood, wit instead of death...

Ilmater, the goddess of air, was bored. Floating about aimlessly in space was no fun.

So, down she dived into the depth of the oceans. And there she lay for 700 long years.

Then from the shell of a golden egg laid on her leg by a duck, Ilmater created the Moon, the Sun and the stars with the Heavens above and Earth below, and yes, the oceans, the islands, the rivers and the mountain cliffs too.

When she was almost done, she finally gave birth to wonderful Vainamoinen, a magical child with superpowers, who then helped create the rest of the world, says the Finnish epic *Kalevala* which means 'Land of Heroes' – which was Finland.

It then invites you to listen to not only the stories of the glorious legends of the past but also the adventures of the wizard Vainamoinen and his brother Ilmarinen.

Not to be left out of the epic are Joukahainen, his sister Aino and the wicked Louhi with her daughters – the Maids of Beauty and Rainbow – as well as Lemminkainen and the evil slave Kullervo.

To begin with, taking the help of birds and water maidens, Vainamoinen scattered seeds of every kind and soon created forested countryside across the land, and then with his *kantele,* a Finnish harp-like stringed instrument, began to sing.

He sang such wonderful songs that his fame spread far and wide. For when he made music, not only did trees dance and rivers rise in sheer joy, but birds too kept time and beasts were calmed while happiness filled the hearts of men.

Then, one day, as he roamed the countryside singing his enchanting songs, a boastful young man called Joukahainen from the Northland (Lapland) came to him. Having heard of Vainamoinen's fame, Joukahainen challenged him to a singing duel.

As they showed off their singing skills and warbled about who created the world and competed on all kinds of topics, the arrogant Joukahainen found himself losing.

So, as he reached for his sword to strike Vainamoinen, wise Vainamoinen told him, 'Defeat me with your words not your sword,' and vanquished him with just the enchanting power of his songs.

The magic in his chants was so powerful that Joukahainen's sledge and harness melted, and he was pulled down into treacherous quicksand.

A desperate Joukahainen begged Vainamoinen, 'Please save me. Pull me out of this sand. I promise you the hand of my lovely sister Aino if you help me live.'

So, an unmarried but older Vainamoinen took pity on him.

Again, with the power of his songs, he loosened the quicksand around Joukahainen and helped him jump out alive.

Thus began Vainamoinen's many hair-raising adventures, including the fruitless search for a wife.

•••

Joukahainen's parents were thrilled at the idea of the famed Vainamoinen as a son-in-law. Aino was not.

Bribed by her mother with expensive ornaments and gifts, she preferred to take them off and plunge into the sea rather than marry an old man, however wise and magical he might be.

No one dared tell her parents the sad news. Not the bears nor the foxes or the birds who saw her dive and drown.

As her blood turned into a river and her ribs into willows, her hair into seagrass and her flesh into fish, a hare on the threat of being roasted alive by the sea maidens, finally delivered the bad news.

Poor old Vainamoinen was heartbroken.

'Go search for a bride further afield,' ordered Vainamoinen's mother and so, while he did that, Joukahainen tried to kill him with a crossbow to avenge his sister's death.

Then, as Vainamoinen was flailing in the sea, the Maid of Beauty rescued him.

Now, Beauty's mother, Louhi, was the formidable wizard ruler of Pohjola of faraway Northland.

Louhi, impressed with him, promised Vainamoinen Beauty's hand in marriage, if he would build her the 'Sampo', a magic machine that spun out gold and silver.

'I canot,' said Vainamoinen, but eager to marry Beauty, promised to go home and get his brother Ilmarinen, who was a blacksmith, to do so.

His brother, however, was not willing.

So, Vainamoinen caused a powerful storm to blow Ilmarinen all the way to Pohjola, where he had no option but to build Louhi the magical Sampo.

However, the Maid of Beauty refused to marry Vainamoinen and Vainamoinen was disappointed a second time in his quest for a wife.

With the riches churned out by the Sampo, the kingdom of Pohjola was soon wealthy and prosperous.

So Louhi invited Ilmarinen to marry her daughter Beauty instead.

The Maid of Beauty refused him too and a disappointed Ilmarinen decided to go home in a copper boat magically produced by Louhi.

•••

Now, Vainamoinen, who was also building a boat to go home, was being helped by one Lemminkainen.

This Lemminkainen was also in love with the Maid of Beauty. So, he whisked her away and married her.

They stayed married till such time as they broke promises made to each other. He then deserted her.

Lemminkainen now wanted to marry Louhi's second daughter, the Maid of Rainbow. Louhi said no and instead set him some impossible tasks.

While trying to accomplish those tasks, Lemminkainen was killed and then dumped into the River of Death.

Lemminkainen's mother soon came looking for him.

She discovered his slain body parts, put them together and brought him back to life.

With her lilting songs, of course. How else?

Lemminkainen then went home.

Meanwhile, searching for the magic formula to complete building his boat, which only a huge giant knew, Vainamoinen found himself inside the giant's stomach till he was spat out, along with the formula!

He finished building the boat and told Louhi, 'I want to marry the Maid of Rainbow.' Apparently Ilmarinen too desired to do the same.

Though Louhi again favoured Vainamoinen, the Maid of Rainbow preferred the younger Ilmarinen.

So Vainamoinen, refused by Aino, Beauty and now Rainbow, was disappointed for the third time.

●●●

A peeved Lemminkainen who had, if you remember, wanted to marry Rainbow too after he left Beauty, was not invited to Rainbow and Ilmarinen's wedding.

So, he set out to take revenge. However, Louhi froze the seas and Lemminkainen was forced to turn back.

Enter Kullervo, the son of Evil, who had been sold as a slave to Ilmarinen.

Ill-treated by Rainbow, Ilmarinen's new wife, Kullervo, in no time, had the wolves and the bears kill her.

A sad and wife-less Ilmarinen then forged himself another wife, one of gold and silver, but found her cold and lifeless.

He offered her to Vainamoinen, who, even though he was still without a wife, said no.

Ilmarinen then carried away another of Louhi's daughters, but she was so unhappy with him, he turned her into a seagull.

A disappointed Ilmarinen now remembered the Sampo.

So, the three of them – Vainamoinen, Ilmarinen and Lemminkainen – got together and decided they would steal the Sampo.

'After all,' said Ilmarinen, 'I created it.'

So, while Vainamoinen sang and put everyone in Pohjola to sleep, they stole the Sampo from its hiding place in the mountains.

Louhi, however, realizing what they were up to, turned herself quickly into an eagle.

Then, leading a huge army, she attacked them and, in the tussle, the Sampo fell into the sea and was lost.

Now, an angry Louhi, using her song-magic, visited all kinds of problems on them including diseases, as well as – guess what! – bears to eat them up. All of which Vainamoinen, with his powerful music, easily thwarted.

Vainamoinen next came across an unmarried Marjatta whose infant son he felt had to be killed.

WHO WROTE IT AND WHY

Elias Lonrott, a doctor, wrote *The Kalevala* after as many as eleven song-collecting field trips across the country. He compiled some 22,795 verses of fifty chapters or cantos from 2,000-year-old Finnish ballads and lyrical songs. *The Kalevala* was first published in 1835 and then in expanded form in 1849, and remains Finland's immensely popular national epic.

Lonrott was born on 9 April 1802 in Sammatti, Finland. With a medical degree in 1833 from the University of Helsinki, he became a district medical officer at Kajanni in eastern Finland. During his two-decade stay there, he went on field trips to Sami, where he met the Estonian and the Finnish tribes of north-western Russia and began collecting chants, fables, riddles, proverbs and folktales, and converted them into this popular literary epic that it became. Recognized for his efforts, he was made professor of Finnish language and literature at the University of Helsinki (1853–62). He also compiled the first Finnish–Swedish dictionary during 1866–80. The impact of his works was so massive that *The Kalevala* was possibly among the works that inspired J.R.R. Tolkien's *The Silmarillion* and *The Lord of the Rings*.

His other notable works: *Kanteletar* (1840), a collection of Finnish folk poetry.

However, when the little infant, who later grew up to become King of Karelia and Finland, plaintively asked him why, old Vainamoinen was remorseful.

Then leaving his *kantele* behind, he wearily sailed away for good in his boat, saying, 'I will return to sing new songs when the time is right,' thus bringing to an end the epic adventures of the colourful heroes of Kalevala.

Celebrating 28 February as Kalevala Day, almost everything in Finland – from rock bands to classical recitals and banks to distilleries – display The Kalevala *as their inspiration in various forms.*

EL CANTAR DE MIO CID

...And so, with great valour, fought the great warrior and nobleman El Cid, to restore his lost honour and place in society.

There were no fiery dragons nor winged steeds. No nymph-like goddesses nor helpful Olympian gods.

No powerful magic, no death-defying chants. Nor was he a superhero.

El Cid's life was an open book and yet it was the kind that legends were made of.

Called upon to defend his father's honour at a tender age, he not only defended it but cut off the enemy's head and produced it before his father as proof.

Then, slaying five attacking Moorish kings all at once, Rodrigo Diaz of Vivar rose to fame to be known forever more as 'El Cid', or 'The Lord'.

Growing up in the royal Spanish court of Ferdinand I of Castile, El Cid was not only loyal to the old king but also to the monarch's two sons who ruled after him.

An able lieutenant to Sancho, the eldest, till he was killed, El Cid then loyally served the younger brother Alfonso, who succeeded Sancho.

He even rose from his sickbed to win for Alfonso a resounding victory over powerful enemies knocking at the gates.

However, unfortunately, his successes in the field caused a lot of heartburn and jealousy among the king's courtiers.

'He is trying to overthrow you, sire,' they said, and King Alfonso VI of Castile immediately felt threatened.

Then accusing El Cid of robbing the treasury, they foisted a false case on him.

Not waiting to hear his defence, Alfonso used that as an excuse to exile El Cid.

He summarily banished him from the country forthwith. To be gone immediately. Within nine days, if you please, at the risk of being put to death if he tarried any longer. Not even allowing him the usual thirty days usually given to a criminal.

Warning people against helping him at the risk of death, Alfonso stripped him of his titles and lands as well.

So it was that when El Cid went home, he found his own door closed to him.

Shocked, he stood awhile outside his home.

However, when no one dared speak for fear of punishment, a little girl bravely stepped forward to tell

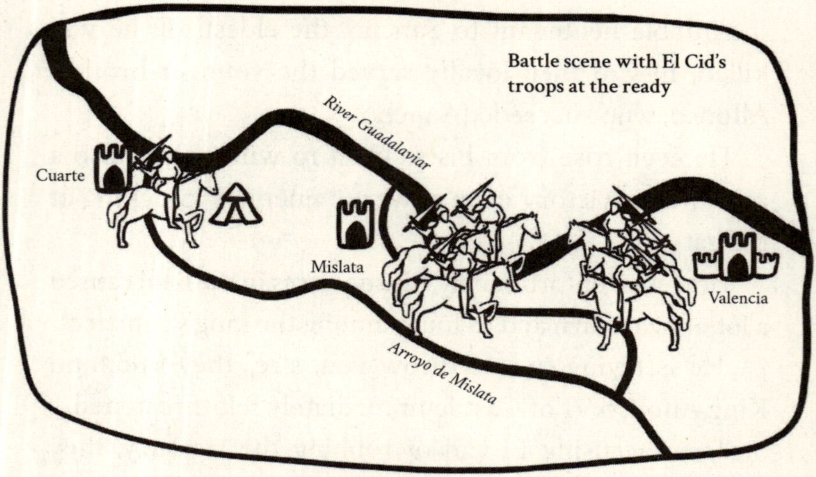

him that they had been told their lives would be at stake if they were to help him.

An indignant El Cid turned around and went outside the gates. He then camped on a neighbouring hill.

He was quickly joined by his cousin and, one by one, many courtiers loyal to him came out, and slowly their band grew. Soon, he had a tidy little army all of his own.

Then he bade his wife and two little girls goodbye at a nearby monastery, promising to be back to avenge his humiliation and restore his honour.

Thus began the legendary exploits of El Cid and his band of brave men.

●●●

Fighting one gallant battle after another successfully, El Cid began to win much fame and acclaim.

He conquered nearby kingdoms and unified them under him.

Without laying waste to them and ruling wisely, he started to amass great wealth as well.

Winning the respect of all those whom he conquered, he soon came to be both feared and admired.

However, never once did he try to usurp King Alfonso's throne.

Instead, with every conquest, a caravan of riches and horses would always be sent to the king at Castile.

Even after a particularly long and successful conquest of Valencia, the stronghold of the Muslim Moors, his loyalty to Alfonso remained intact.

He was, however, forced to endure, for many years, the humiliation of not being allowed to return home.

•••

Then one day, King Alfonso, hearing of El Cid's heroic war exploits, decided to forgive him.

He invited El Cid back home to Castile and offered to have his two young nephews marry the two young daughters of El Cid.

El Cid could have spurned the offer and declared himself king of an independent Valencia.

However, he did neither, and though a bit wary of the idea, reluctantly agreed to the match, and came back.

The girls were soon married to the young princes. They were content, and so was El Cid for a while.

Till one day, on a campaign trail, a lion attacked their camp.

The gutless sons-in-law ran away in fear while El Cid managed to capture the lion and cage him.

Ridiculed by El Cid's men for their lack of courage, the princes felt humiliated.

Deciding to take revenge, they ill-treated their young wives, left them by the roadside and returned home.

The girls were, however, rescued and El Cid filed a case against the princes.

Alfonso, shocked at the boys' barbaric behaviour, permitted the court case to go ahead.

'Give me back the two jewel-encrusted swords I gave you as part of their dowry,' demanded El Cid.

The two cowardly princes returned them.

'Now, return the gold I settled on you at the time of the wedding,' he said.

The gold was long gone, but they quickly gave up property in lieu.

Still not satisfied, El Cid challenged them to a duel and defeated them.

His family honour thus restored, El Cid was content. In the meanwhile, two emissaries from the powerful kingdoms of Aragon and Navarre arrived.

They wanted El Cid's daughters as brides for their future kings.

To their joy, permission was granted.

His daughters would now be queens while their former husbands would return home in disgrace.

Thus, his own honour now restored, El Cid was a happy man.

Time passed. El Cid realized he did not have much longer to live.

Valencia was being attacked by the Moors again.

El Cid knew that without him, Valencia would not be able to hold out.

So, he prepared his men for the inevitable.

He told them that if after his death the Moors should attack, 'Then embalm my body, lift me up onto my horse, bind me to it and, with soldiers flanking me, make me ride through the enemy files to carry on straight to my home in Castile where I may finally be laid to rest.'

A few days later, El Cid passed away.

So, believing he was dead, the Moors attacked. However, they were shocked to see an erect El Cid bearing down upon them.

WHO WROTE IT AND WHY

El Cid's tale is said to have been told by a wandering minstrel in 1140 CE, or perhaps later by one Per Abbad around the thirteenth century (1207) CE in some 3,700 lines of two cantos. Considered to be Spain's national epic, *El Cantar de Mio Cid* or 'The Song of my Lord' is based on El Cid's life that begins with his banishment and ends with his death in 1099 CE.

Convinced he was still alive, they panicked, broke rank and ran away.

This was to be the gallant El Cid's last victory.

Laid to rest just as he wanted in the monastery of San Pedro de Cardena in Castile, El Cid's fame and glory lives on, nine centuries later.

Always well-dressed, El Cid sported a beard so long that it needed to be tied up with satin ribbons! He was immensely proud of it.

THE EPIC OF GILGAMESH

When a demigod went in search of immortality...

'Go up on the wall of Uruk and walk around,
Examine its foundation, inspect its brickwork thoroughly.
Is not even the core of the brick structure made of kiln-fired brick,
And did not the Seven Sages themselves lay out its plans?
One league city, one league palm gardens, one league lowlands, the open area of the Ishtar Temple,
Three leagues and the open area of Uruk the wall encloses.'

– *The Epic of Gilgamesh, I, 16–21; XI, 312–319*

The description of a nineteenth-century city with gardens and temples, you think? Or maybe a town just a bit earlier, in the medieval times perhaps?

No. Guess again.

It is a city built in the second century BCE, on the River Euphrates in ancient Sumer in southern Mesopotamia, thousands of years ago. (Now the region falls in south-central Iraq.)

It is also how the world's oldest *Epic of Gilgamesh* starts and ends.

So, what and who was Gilgamesh?

Gilgamesh was the king of Uruk. He was apparently part man and part god.

So, he had all the powers of a superman and some more.

He could lift mountains and fight monsters with such ease that he became a wee bit arrogant.

Although he was a good king, he thought too highly of himself. He treated his subjects with contempt.

So, to curb his arrogance, the gods, heeding the wishes of his people, created Enkidu, a faster and stronger man, wild enough to challenge Gilgamesh.

They fashioned him out of clay, dressed him up in human clothes and introduced him to the ways of the human world.

Enkidu then went looking for Gilgamesh.

He soon found him and challenged him to a fight.

They wrestled each other ferociously till Gilgamesh managed to throw him to the ground in such a way that Enkidu had no option but to admit defeat.

However, when they shook hands, they found they liked each other, and so ended up being great friends for the rest of their lives.

The two of them then began to go on adventures together, which is what the epic is all about.

●●●

'Let's take on Humbaba, the monster who guards the Cedar Forest where no humans are allowed,' said Gilgamesh one day.

'No,' said the people of Uruk. 'You will certainly be killed.'

'Yes,' said Enkidu, jumping up.

So, off they went to fight Humbaba, ignoring the wishes of the people.

As they neared his habitat, Humbaba came to the forest edge, roaring at them.

A terrific battle took place, and just as Gilgamesh was about to put a knife through Humbaba, the latter begged for his life.

As Gilgamesh hesitated, Enkidu yelled, 'Finish him off, Gilgamesh. Finish him off. He cannot be allowed to live.'

So, an angry and desperate Humbaba cursed Enkidu, 'In an early death, you shall die.'

Hearing these unfortunate words for his friend, a furious Gilgamesh did not wait any more.

Without further ado, he plunged the knife into Humbaba, killing him instantly.

Upset with the curse but holding Humbaba's head aloft, they went home in triumph, only to bump into the goddess Ishtar.

Ishtar, who was interested in Gilgamesh, tried to be friendly but Gilgamesh who was not interested, spurned her friendly gestures.

Furious, she called upon the Bull of Heaven to gore him to death.

The bull, looking for Gilgamesh, unleashed such a reign of terror among the people that even the gods were left shocked.

However, Enkidu – with Gilgamesh – managed to kill it.

It was now Ishtar's turn to curse Enkidu, and soon a depressed, doubly cursed Enkidu fell ill.

He had such terrible dreams that he knew he was dying, and a grieving Gilgamesh promised to erect a statue of gold in his memory, after his death.

●●●

After Enkidu died, a grief-stricken Gilgamesh asked the birds and the trees, the rivers and the fish and everyone else to mourn him, and then began to ponder over 'death' and 'immortality'.

'I am a man like Enkidu. I will also die one day, won't I? Can't I live forever?' he wondered and decided to look up Utnapishtim, an ancestor of his who had defied death and was immortal.

Thus began Gilgamesh's journey to find immortality.

In search of Utnapishtim, he fought off many dangers of the kind only a demigod could overcome.

He first met two half-scorpion beings on top of the Mashu Mountain, who allowed him to pass only after hearing his sorrowful tale of Enkidu's death and his need to find why it had happened.

He then wandered through a tunnel of darkness for days before bursting out into a garden of brilliant dazzling gems. There, Siduri, the gods' tavern keeper, tried to warn him to return home. However, seeing his determination, she finally directed him to cross the dangerous oceans to meet Urshanabi, the ferryman of the gods.

Urshanabi also tried to frighten Gilgamesh into going back, before agreeing to ferry him across the River of Death.

'If you survive it,' he said, 'you will meet Utnapishtim.'

An undeterred Gilgamesh survived, to stumble upon Utnapishtim, who asked, 'Gilgamesh, why are you here? Death is inevitable. Only gods are immortal.'

Gilgamesh was, however, not dissuaded. He insisted on knowing Utnapishtim's secret to eternal life.

'I was warned of a great flood that would end the world,' said Utnapishtim, 'so I built a boat, gathered my family and as many animals as I could and got on board. For six days and seven days did it rain, till finally all drowned except those of us on the boat. On the seventh day when the Sun shone bright, we went outside and began living anew.'

So, 'Go sleepless for six days and seven nights,' Gilgamesh was told. 'You fill find the secret to eternal life.'

However, Gilgamesh wasn't able to stay awake. He promptly fell asleep.

Distraught and defeated, Gilgamesh was about to go home when Utnapishtim's wife, feeling sorry for him, told her husband, 'At least give him the secret to eternal youth.'

WHO WROTE IT AND WHY

Inscribed initially by Gilgamesh himself, only twelve clay tablets, dated to the seventh century BCE, with about 2,000 lines in cuneiform (an ancient form of writing) have been found describing around five of his adventures. Woven into a linked narrative of *The Epic of Gilgamesh* in the Akkadian language by poet Sin-leqi-unninni of Babylon in the second century BCE, it is supposedly the oldest epic in the world.

Gilgamesh, a king of Uruk, an ancient city of Sumer and later of Babylonia, probably ruled for 126 years during the Early Dynastic Period, between c. 2900 and 2350 BCE. Fragments of his life are picked up from archaic texts and inscriptions, but not much can be said with certainty. He appears to live as a mythic legend in the hearts of the people.

Tablet V of the epic

'There is a plant many fathoms deep in the ocean,' Utnapishtim told Gilgamesh. 'If you can get it, you will always be young. But many a danger needs to be overcome to reach it.'

A determined Gilgamesh then dived into the sea, fought off a horrible giant octopus among other dangers, found the plant and came up for air.

Then bidding Utnapishtim and his wife goodbye, he happily set out for Uruk and home.

On the way, he went for a swim, leaving the plant on the beach. A snake, attracted by its perfume, crawled up and swallowed the plant whole.

Poor Gilgamesh came ashore to find the plant gone and only the shed skin of the snake lying around.

Unhappily, he realized that there was no power on Earth that would make him immortal or permanently young.

Going back home with the ferryman Urshanabi, Gilgamesh took Urshanabi around Uruk to glumly realize that, 'My kingdom is actually my legacy of immortality.'

Thus ends the story of Gilgamesh.

Discovered from among the ruins of the Library of Ashurbanipal in Nineveh, the Assyrian capital, the tablets were shipped to a London museum in 1872. A curator called George Smith, who had a keen interest in cuneiform since his youth, was overjoyed at being able to decipher some of the lines, especially about the floods – he was so delighted that he began stripping off his clothes excitedly.

THE ODYSSEY

The return journey of a Greek hero...

Polyphemus, the ugly, one-eyed giant Cyclops, waited.

He saw the sailors wash up ashore and wander into his cave.

He then grabbed them one by one.

Sinking his teeth gleefully into their juicy flesh, he went chomp, chomp, chomp.

He had devoured half a dozen and more before a desperate Odysseus managed to sharpen a stake and thrust it into his eye.

As the blinded and raging one-eyed giant howled and danced in pain, clever Odysseus and his band of sailors quickly made their escape.

Guarding a narrow strait were the rock sea monsters Scylla and Charybdis.

'Avoid the man-eating sea monsters Scylla and Charybdis,' Odysseus had been told, 'but if you can't, go closer to the twelve-footed Scylla with her six snaking tentacles ending in sharp-toothed heads, because she can only devour six men at a time while Charybdis, the whirlpool monster, can sink a whole ship.'

So, as they passed the narrow straits, Scylla's dozen snarling tentacles snaked out. They grabbed Odysseus's men. As they writhed, gasped, screamed and flailed their arms about, trying to escape, Scylla swung them up her cliff and into her huge, cavernous mouth to swallow them whole.

Who was Odysseus? And why was he facing such perilous encounters?

Odysseus was the king of Ithaca.

He was also a wily man.

The Trojan War with Troy had dragged on for ten long years. Brave Achilles was dead, so was Patroclus, and many other Greek heroes had suffered the same fate.

Who knew if he himself was next? He needed to bring the war to an end.

So, he devised a neat little trick. He built a large wooden horse and filled it with soldiers.

Then leaving it behind on the shores outside the city of Troy, Odysseus ordered his Greek ships to pretend they were going back to Greece and park themselves out of sight a few nautical miles away.

So, unaware of the hidden Greek soldiers and fooled into believing that the Greeks had gone home leaving the horse as a victory gift for them, the Trojans dragged the horse through the gates into Troy, doing exactly what Odysseus had hoped for.

The Greek warriors then jumped out of the horse at night and stealthily opened the gates.

Their fellow soldiers stationed away from the shore came in, took the Trojans by surprise and massacred all of them, thereby winning the war and bringing it to an end.

●●●

Victorious but weary, the Greeks now began to return home, one by one. So did Odysseus.

However, it took him as long as the war itself, another ten long years, beset with peril and aided a lot by the gods. At last, he reached Ithaca where his wife Queen

Penelope and son Telemachus, unaware if he was alive or dead, waited in hope.

And it was in the course of that long, perilous journey home that he had many death-defying encounters.

Odysseus first sailed to the island of the Cicones.

Blown off course by a tremendous storm, he and his men were forced to land on the Lotus Eaters' island where, thanks to memory-sapping plants, they were put in a state of stupor.

Pulling themselves away, they somehow reached the land of Cyclops, the one-eyed giant from where, as you know, Odysseus managed to escape.

Unfortunately, this Cyclops happened to be the son of the sea god Poseidon.

So, just when they were in sight of Ithaca, thanks to an angry Poseidon, Odysseus's entire fleet was tossed, turned and ferociously buffeted around by stormy winds and tall waves, all the way back to right where they had started.

They rowed out again. This time, a tribe of cannibalistic Laestrygonians sank their ships.

Shipless, they were forced onto the island of the enchantress Circe, who put a spell on them.

She turned them into pigs.

Managing, however, to lift her spell, they got their human forms back and escaped, only to have to desperately save themselves from the singing sea nymphs, the Sirens, who with their lilting songs wickedly lured unsuspecting sailors to dash against their rocks and die.

On to the narrow Strait of Messina, where again as you know, they lost six more men to Scylla but somehow managed to avoid Charybdis, only to lose more men to an angry Zeus whose cattle had been eaten by Odysseus's men.

A furious Zeus killed all of them except Odysseus.

Odysseus was then washed ashore Ogygia, the island of the sea nymph goddess Calypso, where he was stranded for the next half a dozen years and more.

Held captive by Calypso on the island, Odysseus was unable to leave.

●●●

Meanwhile, in Ithaca, Penelope and Telemachus were having trouble.

With Odysseus gone for twenty years and no knowledge of his whereabouts, there were many traitorous courtiers who believed that Odysseus was dead.

They aspired for Penelope's hand and were constantly trying to get her to marry one of them. They also didn't want Telemachus around.

However, Penelope loved her husband and was convinced that he would be back someday.

'I will marry one of you once I finish weaving this burial shroud for Odysseus's father Laertes,' Penelope said, and bought herself some time by weaving it during the day and secretly unravelling it by night.

Hoping for some news of his father, a desperate Telemachus decided to meet the survivors of the Trojan War.

To his joyful relief, he was told, 'Yes, your father is alive. He survived the war and must be trying to get back home.'

Just about then, the gods decided to free Odysseus from Calypso's reluctant clutches.

He was therefore allowed to escape, but a vengeful Poseidon shipwrecked him once again, to have him washed ashore Scheria, the land of the Phaeacians, ruled by King Alcinous.

Odysseus narrated to them his adventures right up to how he landed up in Scheria, and was treated royally and promised help to return to Ithaca.

Goddess Athena now stepped in to aid Odysseus.

She outwitted Poseidon, calmed the waves, and helped a happy and relieved Odysseus reach Ithaca.

In Ithaca, Odysseus, worried that Penelope's suitors might kill him if they knew who he was, disguised himself as a beggar.

Nobody recognized him but for his old dog. Mad with joy, the animal kicked up such a ruckus that Odysseus's old nurse came to see what was happening, and she recognized him too.

WHO WROTE IT AND WHY

The Greek poet Homer wrote the epic around the eighth or seventh century BCE in 12,109 lines divided into twenty-four books corresponding to the letters of the Greek alphabet. 'Odyssey' meaning 'long journey' and the tale, covering the last six weeks of Odysseus's journey home, is a sequel to Homer's *The Iliad* and among the oldest existing works of literature still read and studied by students even today. Books 1–4 focuses on Telemachus, Penelope and the nasty suitors while books 5–8 deal with Odysseus's escape to the Phaeacians. In books 9–21, Odysseus narrates his adventures to the Phaeacians and books 22–24 describe the killing of the suitors and the reunion of Odysseus and Penelope.

His Muses: All nine Muses, the daughters of Zeus.

He swore her to secrecy, and with the help of a loyal swineherd, went to meet an overjoyed Telemachus.

Telemachus himself had, thanks to Athena, just escaped an ambush to kill him by the treacherous suitors.

Then followed a shooting tournament.

'Anyone who wishes to marry me must string the great bow of Odysseus and shoot an arrow through a ring of twelve axes as he used to,' announced Penelope, who was unaware that Odysseus was back home.

As they all failed, the beggar stepped forward.

Not only did he shoot the arrows straight through the ring, but he also shot every one of those arrogant and troublesome courtiers as well – through the heart.

When she heard news of the killings, 'Could it really be him,' wondered Penelope in disbelief and hope.

However, she was still not sure.

So, to test Odysseus, she asked her men, 'Could you do me a favour and move my bed out of here?'

It was a strange request, but to her utter delight Odysseus asked rather angrily in reply, 'Why? Wasn't our bed made with the wood of the tree I struck down?' This was a secret only he and she knew.

Ecstatic, she hugged him.

Thus, the epic story of Odysseus's long journey home came to an end and he was happily reunited with his wife Penelope.

The Odyssey *is filled with omens. When two eagles tear each other to death, it meant death for the suitors, while when an eagle with a goose in its claws or a hawk with a dove flew by, it was seen as a good omen.*

THE AENEID

The story of the escape from Troy and the beginnings of Rome...

Aeneas woke up with a start. Was he hallucinating? Had Hector actually spoken to him just now?

'Leave. Get out fast,' Hector had said.

Such great friends and comrades-in-arms they had been, until Achilles the Greek warrior had killed Hector in the Trojan War.

Wide awake now, Aeneas realized it had indeed been a dream.

Well, dead or alive, if Hector was telling him to escape, escape he would.

Anyway, the war was lost, and his city of Troy was on fire.

So, Aeneas gathered his family around, picked up his ailing father and ran out of the burning city.

Guided by the gods, he decided to set sail in search of a new homeland. To start a new life.

Aeneas then rode the same seas, faced the same dangers and had the same gods fight over him as Odysseus, who had sought to return home after the Trojan War, Jason who had gone looking for the Golden Fleece, and Vasco da Gama who had set sail for India long, long after them all.

Aeneas, however, wasn't to know that the goddess Juno disliked all Trojans, and Aeneas in particular.

Why? Because...

- Her arch-rival goddess Aphrodite (also known as Venus) had been declared to be the fairest of them all by Paris, a Trojan prince.
- Her husband, Jupiter, the king of gods, had replaced her daughter Hebe with Ganymede, another Trojan prince, as the gods' special cup-bearer.
- Her favourite city of Carthage was now prophesied to be destroyed by yet another Trojan and a war hero at that, one who was destined to found a whole new city called Rome. That hero was Aeneas.
- Who was Aeneas? He was none other than the son of her enemy, the goddess Venus.

And Juno could do nothing about it. Or could she? She could at least try, she decided angrily.

Now as he ran, Aeneas realized his dear wife was missing. He went back for her, only to have her ghost tell him to not look for her but leave quickly.

So, returning to his ship, they quickly set sail to dock first at Thrace where the spirits bade him to carry on to Delos.

At Delos, the priest now ordered him, 'Go on to where your ancestors are. It is your final destination. The gods have decided.'

En route, encountering those horrible half-bird–half-women Harpies whom they somehow managed to escape, they reached Epirus where Aeneas was pleasantly surprised to meet Hector's widow, Andromache, as he hadn't expected to bump into her.

Queen though she was of Epirus, she was still mourning her dead husband.

While she encouraged them to carry on, Aeneas also learned that it was predicted that he would eventually settle in Italy.

Bidding goodbye to Andromache, they sailed via the narrow straits guarded by the six-headed, twelve-footed, snake-necked Scylla and the whirlpool monster Charybdis, who strangely did them no harm, and on to Drepanum in Sicily where, heartbreakingly, his father Anchises died.

Giving him a funeral befitting a king, they continued to sail on when Juno now began to make life difficult for Aeneas.

First with the help of the wind gods, she whipped up a storm. A squall so fierce that it threw Aeneas completely off course.

He lost his men and his fleet of ships.

However, with the help of his mother Venus and the sea god Neptune, he – unfortunately for Juno – landed on – you guessed it! – Carthage.

Thanks to his mother again, there in the harbour, to his joy, were his missing ships as well.

Carthage was incredibly beautiful and so was her lovely queen, Dido.

Dazzled by the city and welcomed warmly by Dido, Aeneas spent many a happy day in her company as he narrated to her the entire story of the Trojan War.

'We were defeated by a wooden horse filled with Greek soldiers who destroyed Troy,' he said. 'We thought we had won the war and brought the horse into our city, only to be massacred in our sleep. The Greek warrior Achilles's son killed our old king Priam before my very eyes. So, gathering my family, I escaped with my mother Venus's help.'

The two soon fell in love, and now loath to leave Carthage, Aeneas went on to tell her the reason for his flight and his search for a new place to settle.

He even described his journey on the seas thus far and the terrible storm that had finally brought him to her.

As he lingered on in Carthage, the gods who were watching his every move, were quick to remind him, 'This is not your final destination. Do not tarry in Carthage any longer, Aeneas. Leave immediately.'

Despite a heartbroken Dido pleading with him to stay, afraid to displease the gods, he prepared to set sail again.

He departed quickly, without even bidding her goodbye and unbeknown to him, a grief-stricken Dido killed herself.

●●●

Aeneas sailed on. To finally reach Drepanum harbour. Only to have a vengeful Juno set all his ships on fire.

Able to save just a few of the vessels, an upset Aeneas was ready to give up when his father's ghost appeared before him.

'Carry on, Aeneas,' it said, 'to Latium on the Tiber via the underworld, where I will meet you.'

Again, all set to make mischief among the oceans was Juno. So, Neptune promised Venus that he would protect her son.

Aeneas, now on his way to the underworld, met the prophetess Sibyl of Cumae, a priestess who told him, 'Bring me the Golden Bough, the key to the underworld, and I will take you there.'

So, with the help of Venus's doves who got the bough for him, Aeneas delivered the Golden Bough to her.

Now guided by Sibyl in the underworld, he met many of his dead friends and comrades, including Hector.

As promised, his father met him there too. After giving him a potted forecast of Rome's future for the next thousand years, his father sent Aeneas on his way to Latium.

Entering Latium by way of the River Tiber, he was welcomed by King Latinus, whose daughter Lavinia was engaged to Turnus, the prince of a neighbouring kingdom.

So impressed was Latinus by Aeneas that he now wanted Lavinia to marry Aeneas instead of Turnus.

Especially as his soothsayers said that Aeneas was a better match for Lavinia.

Juno now interfered again. This time, in an even more terrible manner.

Sowing discord among them, Juno turned Lavinia's mother, Queen Amata, and Turnus against Aeneas.

A fight seemed inevitable, so Aeneas collected the support of nearby allies while the rest of the kingdoms turned out for Turnus.

Sadly, a war broke out.

Even though Juno knew that the gods had decided Aeneas would triumph, she tried to delay the inevitable.

So, she continued to play mischief.

She even managed to get Aeneas wounded, but Venus cured him with a magic herb.

At one stage when neither side appeared to be winning, Aeneas and Turnus decided to duel one another.

However, another full-scale battle took place.

Constantly aiding and abetting Turnus at every turn, Juno was about to intervene again, when, 'No, stop,' said her husband Jupiter. 'You will stop interfering right now.'

Finally, as Aeneas was by far the superior warrior, he was able to slay Turnus and win the war.

Aeneas then married Lavinia and went on to found the city of Lavinium.

Thus ended, rather abruptly, the epic story of Aeneas's search for a home.

WHO WROTE IT AND WHY

Virgil, a famous Italian poet, wrote *The Aeneid* in 9,896 lines spread over twelve books in Latin, between 29 BCE and 19 BCE to further the image of his Emperor Augustus – Julius Caesar's heir – who wanted the world to see him as directly descended from brave Aeneas and his descendants.

Virgil was born in 70 BCE in Mantua, Italy. He grew up in a farming village but was educated at Milan and Rome. Trained in philosophy, he was believed to have been inspired by Greek and Roman writers. Virgil saw the rise of Emperor Augustus, the first Roman emperor who took over after the destruction of the republic by the dictatorial Julius Caesar, and the enthusiasm that Virgil felt for the revival of Rome is expressed in all his works. *The Aeneid* occupied many years of his life, and though he left it unfinished, every student at the time was required to memorize its 63,000 and more words. Virgil's poetry left a lasting impression in the minds of Romans, and this was reflected in the works of younger poets like Ovid and, further down the line, in those of Edmund Spenser and even John Milton.

His other notable works: The *Georgics* (29 BCE), a poem about agriculture.

His Muses: Goddesses Clio, the Patron of History; Erato, the Muse of Lyric Poetry; and Melpomene, the Muse of Tragedy.

His son, Ascanius, also known as Iulus or Julius, founded Alba Longa, near where Romulus the legendary founder and first king of Rome would eventually lay the foundations of Rome itself.

'No day will erase you from the memory of time,' a quote from The Aeneid, *Book IX, is displayed in what was a New York subway station before the 9/11 attack on the World Trade Center towers, on the wall of the museum dedicated to the victims of the bombing.*

KUMARASAMBHAVAM

And to destroy the demon king Tarakasura was born Karthikeyan the warlord.

Picture this.

The Himalayas in all their wondrous high-peaked beauty.

Sitting in solitary splendour under a *devadaru* tree was Lord Shiva.

Clad in a simple tiger skin, the serpent coiled round his blue neck, he sat in deep meditation.

Around him the freshness of untouched nature. So pure that its fragrance filled the air.

Guarding him was his faithful bull, Nandi. With a golden cane in his hand and a finger to his lips, he stood watch over Shiva.

The bees ceased their humming and the gazelles slept. The birds rested. All was quiet. All was still.

Picturesque and peaceful.

In the meanwhile, elsewhere in the world, the demon king Tarakasura was on a rampage. Running amok, conquering kingdoms and killing those he didn't like.

Why? Simply because he could do so. Lord Brahma, you see, had given him a boon. Tarakasura could not be killed by man or beast. Therefore, enjoying himself to the hilt, he ran riot, destroying everything the universe held sacred.

He even attacked Indra, the lord of the devas, and drove him out of his kingdom, Devaloka.

So off to Lord Brahma the devas went, 'Please, sire, you need to stop Tarakasura now or we will all soon be destroyed.'

'Hmm,' said Brahma, putting on his thinking cap. 'He can only be curbed by someone divine who is born to Shiva. Only that child will have the power to defeat him.'

Shiva, as you know, was meditating.

He had just lost his beloved partner Sati and he was in intense mourning.

No one dared disturb him.

However, Narada, the wandering *muni* who travelled the three worlds, now intervened.

He had a great idea.

He told them about Uma, the stunning daughter of King Himavan of the Himalaya.

'No one will be able to resist her,' he said. 'She is not only beautiful but also a lovely person. In fact, she is Sati herself born again as Uma.'

The devas agreed. 'Yes, how could Shiva not fall in love with her?' they asked themselves.

Said Brahma then, 'Ask the mountain king Himavan if he is willing to give his daughter in marriage to Shiva. A divine child born to them will kill Tarakasura and rid the world of him. If Himavan is agreeable, then send her to Shiva.'

The Himalayan king was only too willing.

So, Uma – otherwise known as Parvati – who was already in love with Shiva, was asked, 'Are you prepared to become Shiva's wife?'

She was delighted and said yes.

However, an over-anxious Indra decided to take matters into his own hands.

He sought the help of his friend Kamadeva, the lord of love.

So, while the beautiful Parvati and her friend Vasanta (Spring) made their way towards the meditating Shiva, Kamadeva got his special love-powered bow and arrow ready.

'One arrow into Shiva, and the moment he sees Parvati, he will lose concentration and fall in love,' he boasted.

So, into the bower filled with tender green creepers and lovely flowering trees guarded by Nandi, he went.

Just as Kamadeva was about to let fly his arrow, Parvati and her friend arrived.

For a fraction of a second, Shiva lost concentration.

Annoyed, his third eye opened. It spied Kamadeva. It flashed fire, and poor Kamadeva, along with his bow and nocked arrow, was instantly reduced to ashes.

Shiva then went back to his meditation with hardly a glance at Parvati.

•••

Rati, Kamadeva's wife, was inconsolable in her grief.

She was about to throw herself onto his pyre when the gods told her he would soon be revived as a spirit.

A disappointed Parvati now told herself that if she was to attract Shiva, she needed to do something drastic.

To her mother's alarm, Parvati then decided to sit in penance herself.

'Why do you need to do that,' asked her mother, 'when all the great gods live in our home?'

Yet Parvati was adamant.

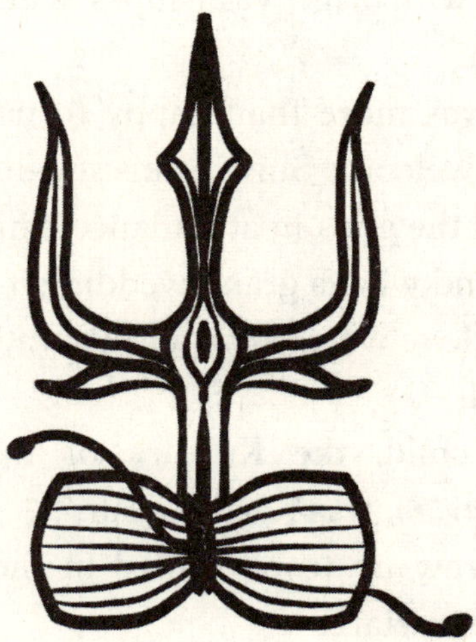

So, through many a winter in freezing water up to her neck and during summers filled with burning fire, she meditated intensely.

Till one day, a sage approached her.

He tried to talk to her about Shiva. He, however, didn't have many nice things to say about him.

So, Parvati told him, 'I don't care. I love him and only him. You can say what you like. It will not change my mind.'

The sage smiled and took on his true form. Miraculously, it was Shiva himself.

Pleased with her reply and her devotion to him, Shiva asked her to marry him, but she told Shiva through her friend, 'Please ask for my father's permission.'

So, Shiva sent the seven sages who stud the sky – the Saptarishis – with Sage Vashishta's wife Arundhati to King Himavan.

The king was more than happy to not only receive them but also welcome Shiva as his son-in-law.

So, with all the gods in attendance, Shiva and Parvati got married, and what a grand wedding it was.

So deep in love were Shiva and Parvati that soon she was with child.

And that child, the Kumara of this epic poem *Kumarasambhavam,* was Karthikeyan.

He soon grew up to be skilled in the art of divine weaponry and warfare.

WHO WROTE IT AND WHY

Kalidasa, the famous Indian poet, composed this epic poem in Sanskrit around the fourth and fifth centuries CE, spread over eight original cantos, said to be a part of 17–22 cantos; the rest was presumed to be added on by others. *Kumarasambhavam* or 'The birth of the war god Kumara' (or Karthikeyan), while not quite in the league of the Ramayana and the Mahabharata or even *Silappadikaram* as an epic, is still considered a beautiful *mahakavya* renowned for its length, brilliant imagery and unmatched literary quality.

His other notable works: *Raghuvamsha*, a poem related to the Raghu dynasty; and *Abhigyanashakuntalam,* a famous Sanskrit play about Shakuntala and King Dushyanta, from the Mahabharata.

Before long, he took up the post for which he was born.

He became the commander-in-chief of the army of the gods.

Added to that, born of Shiva, Karthikeyan was himself powerfully divine as well.

So, when the desperate devas approached him for help, Shiva told Karthikeyan, 'Tarakasura is an enemy of the gods. Son, go take care of him.'

Karthikeyan, riding his magnificent chariot and accompanied by his army of devas, made his way to Tarakasura. Not to be outdone, supported by his demons and with the confidence of one who knew he could not be killed by anybody, Tarakasura went forth to meet his fate.

A mighty battle took place.

Amidst striking thunderbolts and lightning flashes, as the heavens shook and the earth tilted crazily, Karthikeyan killed the devilish Tarakasura and rid the world of a terrible demon that had tried to destroy it.

And with that, so does this epic poem end.

Even as early as the fourth century CE, say global warming experts, Kalidasa in the third canto of this poem has warned us about natural calamities being a fallout of the selfish acts of humans who destroy nature.

BUDDHACHARITA

He who gave up his all, in search of a path to end human suffering...

Have you heard of the prince who gave up his pampered life to become a wandering monk?

It wasn't as if he wasn't handsome, intelligent, loved or popular. He was a prince, after all.

Trained well in all the arts including warfare, there was no royal son as well equipped as he to reign over a kingdom that was both happy and prosperous.

Yet one dark night, he chose to leave his kingdom and home, as also his beautiful wife and bonny son, to steal away.

Why?

One day, the prince, for the very first time in his young life, had spotted an ailing old man.

Shocked at his condition, he had asked, 'What ails him? What is wrong with him?'

He was told, 'It's old age; it comes to everyone.'

'Everyone? To me as well? Does old age always bring suffering?' he then wondered.

The next time he went out, he saw a disease-ridden man.

'What about him?' he asked.

'He is unwell. He is suffering from an illness,' was the answer he got.

'Is "suffering" the source of all problems, then?' questioned the young prince again.

A few days later, he spied a dead body being carried out.

When he was told that this condition was the end for all those who were born on Earth, it made him even more thoughtful about the nature of existence of all humans, their suffering and their end.

'Why does one have to suffer?' he asked himself. 'What is the cause of all this suffering? How does one overcome it?'

Soon after, he came across a meditating monk who had given up everything to lead a simple austere life to find the true path to end all suffering, and discover bliss or happiness.

That made sense to him. 'I too must do that,' he decided, 'and that cannot be found living the kind of pampered life I live right now. I will go into the world, walk its streets and roam its forests to find the true path.'

So, that was why one night he slipped away from his beautiful palace, family and kingdom to a forest nearby.

●●●

He first walked to the kingdom of Magadha whose king offered him his land if he would give up his spiritual quest and go back to being a prince again.

Refusing, he however promised, 'Once I find what I am looking for, I will come back to your kingdom and preach about it.'

He then wandered into the ashram of a great sage.

For the next few years, he lived as a disciple of the seer and practised whatever the great man told him. He learned much from the sage about life, its nature and the reason for living.

However, doing that did not lead him to what he was seeking either.

He asked himself: 'Suffering…what are its causes, why does it happen? How does one end this suffering? What is the right path to break free from this suffering? I need to find it.'

These four points soon came to be known as the four 'Noble Truths': the truth that there is suffering, the truth of the cause of suffering, the truth of the end of suffering, and the truth of the path that can lead to the end of suffering.

He then joined a group of wandering monks who were also looking for an end to suffering, and liberation from the cycle of births and deaths that they believed the soul went through.

They felt that only by denying themselves everything, including food and water, would they find it.

However, following their extremely austere lifestyle, the prince was soon reduced to skin and bones. Yet he hadn't found what he was looking for.

So, he left this group and decided that he needed to find whatever it was, on his own.

●●●

So it was that this young prince, the son of the mighty Sakya king Shuddhodana and Queen Maya of Kapilavastu (now in Nepal), whose name was Siddhartha and at whose birth in Lumbini in the sixth century BCE, the earth itself shook and the Heavens showered flowers, turned into a wandering ascetic. He roamed the country, begging for food till finally, one day, immersed in deep reflection, he sat down in a forest under a *bodhi* tree near the city of Gaya (now in Bihar), and began to meditate.

Many tried to disturb him and frighten him. Angry elephants, tigers, bears and lions were let loose on him. Stones and rocks were flung at him.

In particular, there was a demon called Mara who, it is said in the *Buddhacharita*, with, 'his eyes rolling with rage, lifted up his club at the sage, but the hand holding the club froze.'

Nothing, however, touched the prince. Nothing affected him.

As he meditated, an aura of divinity grew around him. His face shone with a glorious light.

Then, one day, before the crack of dawn, he found the 'knowledge' he had been meditating for.

The Heavens rejoiced, and the gods smiled as enlightenment dawned on the prince.

He realized the truths he had been seeking: 'Life itself is pain or suffering. The path to end this suffering is by rejecting all wants, desires and passions, and having no attachment to anything whatsoever. The power to do so is found in you – in you alone and not in anyone else. That is what will release you from all suffering.'

WHO WROTE IT AND WHY

The *Buddhacharita* or 'The Acts of the Buddha' was written by Indian poet and philosopher Ashvaghosha sometime during the first and second centuries CE in classical Sanskrit. The epic is spread over twenty-eight cantos of which only the first fourteen have survived, although cantos 15–20 exist in the later Tibetan and Chinese (fifth century) versions. The *Buddhacharita*, complete with all of Buddha's teachings, acts as a guide to his followers.

Ashvaghosha, believed to be one of the first dramatists in Sanskrit, was also a monk, philosopher, grammarian and writer. He popularized the Sanskrit poetry style, *kavya*, that involved an elaborate style of writing using similes and metaphors. An excellent orator, Ashvaghosha spoke in great detail about Buddhist philosophy and principles. His fame lay largely in explaining intricate concepts in a simple and subtle way. He travelled across northern India, spreading his wisdom and illuminating people's minds.

His other notable works: *Saundarananda,* a poem about Nanda, Buddha's half-brother.

'So, look into yourself,' he said at his first sermon in Rajagriha in Magadha (now in Bihar). 'You – everyone – has a Buddha or an 'awakened one' within yourself. Find it and you will find the path to overcome suffering and achieve Nirvana or a state of complete peace and happiness.'

Soon the Buddha or the 'Enlightened One', as he came to be known, began to spread the word of his truths across the world.

So, if you want complete happiness, he said, all you need to do is understand the four Noble Truths of Suffering.

Then follow the Middle Path through his Eightfold Path: right view, right thought, right speech, right conduct, right livelihood, right effort, right mindfulness and right meditation, to achieve what that pampered prince who gave up everything to find Nirvana or peace did, says the epic that describes his life and teachings.

Chinese immigrants brought Buddhism to the USA. However, it was their image of a Buddha who was one of their good-luck deities 'Budai' or 'Ch'i-t'zu', who was fat, bald and carrying a sack, that became popular. Soon the 'Laughing Buddha', seen in all Chinese restaurants, who had nothing whatsoever to do with the actual Buddha, became universal.

GERUSALEMME LIBERATA

To deliver the Holy City from Islamic rule did the Crusaders fight a religious war...

'Gabriel,' said God, 'Tell Godfrey to galvanize his men into action. Tell him to go forth at once.'

Godfrey of Bouillon (France) was, however, fast asleep.

His soldiers had captured the cities of Nicaea and Antioch from the Turks and were now camping at Tortosa.

Having been away from home for six long years, he was tired. As were his men.

Now that God had spoken, Gabriel promptly appeared to Godfrey in a dream.

'Godfrey, lead your men to the Holy City,' he said. 'Do not delay.'

Awake, Godfrey immediately called for a war council of other Christian rulers and they decided to waste no time.

Go to war they would, to deliver Jerusalem from the Turks.

Even if it meant fighting to kill all non-believers.

After all, they were the Crusaders, weren't they? And the main purpose of their crusade or mission was to recover the Holy Land, the land of Christ, for their Church.

However, in Jerusalem, at the time, Sultan Aladine, the Islamic ruler of the Holy City, was presiding over a case of a missing statue of the Virgin Mary.

'Who stole the statue?' he thundered and as he enjoyed persecuting Christians, 'Whoever stole it, better own up. If you don't, I will have all Christians in the city, without exception, executed,' he declared.

Suddenly, 'I did it. I stole the Virgin Mary,' said a scared voice from amongst the crowd. It was Sophoronia, a Christian maid, prepared to sacrifice herself to prevent innocent Christians from being killed.

'Let her be burned to death at the stake,' decreed Aladine heartlessly.

As she was being led to the stake, another Christian youth, Olindo, stood up to declare, 'No, sire, it was I who stole the Virgin Mary.'

He wanted to save Sophoronia, whom he was in love with.

'Let them both be burned at the stake,' ordered the Sultan angrily.

Only to be thwarted once again, by Clorinda, a beautiful warrior born of African parents, who was visiting Jerusalem.

'None of the Christians are responsible,' she pleaded, making a special request to save the accused, and then to distract Aladine, offered to fight for him.

Aladine was distracted. He hesitated, then agreed to free the couple but insisted on banishing all the Christians from the city at once, as punishment.

●●●

Meanwhile, two Egyptian emissaries met Godfrey. They sought to prevent him from attacking Jerusalem.

'No, Argante,' said Godfrey to one of them. 'It's my God's will. Jerusalem will be taken.'

True to his words, Godfrey's army was soon knocking at Sultan Aladine's gates.

So, brave Clorinda went out to fight and got into a skirmish with Tancred, one of Godfrey's able lieutenants.

Hard pressed to save himself, Tancred, in the midst of the battle, suddenly discovered that the fearless duelling warrior was a woman. Overwhelmed, he fell blindly in love with her.

Clorinda, however, was not keen, but another Muslim maiden, Erminia, the princess of Antioch, having seen Tancred earlier and secretly fallen in love with him, was very interested.

Jealous of Clorinda, she even went in search of Tancred, pretending to be Clorinda. However, attacked by his men, she was forced to take refuge with a shepherd's family.

Now, Godfrey, egged on by visions of his God and helped by regular thunderstorms and rain whenever required, doubled his efforts to take Jerusalem.

However, if God was in action, would Satan be far behind?

So, Satan, through the wizard Hydrotes, sent the beautiful sorceress Armida to spread disaffection among the Christian ranks.

Her mission was to make Rinaldo, another of Godfrey's able lieutenants, fall in love with her, kill him, and distract the other soldiers including Godfrey.

She succeeded but she didn't bargain on falling in love with Rinaldo herself.

So, she spared Rinaldo but abducted him and tucked him and a few others away from the action, on a beautiful island.

Godfrey, with a depleted army, was suddenly helpless.

Rinaldo, however, was found with God's help, and brought back to his senses by his men. He was all set to leave Armida's island-garden, when she – with Satan's help – sent a posse of her men after Rinaldo.

Rinaldo, however, again with God's timely help, fighting hard to survive, managed to kill all her warriors.

Clorinda, meanwhile, found herself fighting Tancred again, who then unknowingly wounded her grievously.

Clorinda attacks Tancredi, one of a series of paintings by Italian painter Paolo Domenico Finoglia (c. 1590–1645)

Realizing it was Clorinda that he had fatally wounded, he was beside himself with grief. 'I didn't know it was you,' he told her brokenly.

Clorinda forgave him, and even as she lay dying, a heartbroken Tancred converted Clorinda to Christianity.

Now, Godfrey, hearing that reinforcements were on their way to help the Sultan, decided to carry out an assault on the city walls at once.

He knew that once the Egyptian armies arrived, he would have no chance of taking the city.

So, laying siege to the enchanted forests around the Holy City, he broke the enemy's stranglehold and, with Rinaldo's help, breached the city's walls.

Aladine's men were no pushovers, though. They were equally brave and determined to save their city.

Argante, fighting for the Sultan, found himself in a face-off, and in a fight to the finish, with Tancred.

Tancred managed to kill Argante but was deeply wounded himself.

Now over to the Christian side, to his rescue went Erminia. She bound his wounds with her hair to save him.

Meanwhile, Armida realized that she loved Rinaldo too deeply to kill him. So, she decided to kill herself instead.

Rinaldo, however, stopped her. 'Become a Christian and marry me,' he said.

A lovelorn Armida agreed and joined the Christians.

WHO WROTE IT AND WHY

The famous Italian poet Torquato Tasso wrote *Gerusalemme Liberata* around 1575 CE in 1,917 rhyming stanzas of about 15,336 lines spread over twenty cantos of varying lengths in Italian. *Gerusalemme Liberata*, meaning 'Jerusalem Delivered', covers forty days of the first Crusade (religious war between Christians and Muslims) of 1099 in a fictional account.

Torquato Tasso was born in 1544 CE in the Italian city of Sorrento to a poor nobleman, the poet Bernardo Tasso. However, after his father accepted a place in the Court of Urbino in 1557 CE, Torquato grew up in an atmosphere of luxury. Educated along with the Duke's son, he studied law in Padua and was soon an acknowledged philosopher and critic. Young, handsome and cultured, he became popular as a brilliant poet too. *Gerusalemme Liberata* has many plot elements and characters similar to Ariosto's *Orlando Furioso* and was hugely successful. Unfortunately, due to mental health problems, Tasso was soon confined to an asylum and died before he could be crowned poet laureate of Italy.

His other notable works: *Re Torrismondo* (1587 CE), a tragedy which tells the story of Princess Alvida of Norway who is married off against her will; and *Dialoghi* or 'Dialogues' (1578–94 CE), texts covering different issues.

Then the Egyptians arrived and a terrible battle took place.

Godfrey ruthlessly slaughtered his way through the rank and file of his opponent's armies.

After all, he was fighting for his Church, wasn't he?

Even as their enemy soldiers were cut down one by one, it was not as if the Christian soldiers didn't die.

Many of them lost their lives too.

Godfrey, however, with his God on his side, won the day.

The Egyptians were defeated, the Sultan was completely overpowered and Jerusalem was liberated.

With that the epic of *Gerusalemme Liberata* too comes to an end.

While not taught in any boys' schools, Tasso was, however, part of the syllabus in most girls' schools in nineteenth-century Britain...who knows why; perhaps it was due to the presence of the three daring and adventurous women in the epic.

THE EPIC OF SUNDIATA KEITA

Where rivers were of gold and pavements encrusted with gems, the land of the Hakuna Matata...

Who hasn't heard of the Walt Disney film, *The Lion King*, right?

However, did you know that it was loosely based on the life of an African ruler?

That the Lion King was actually Sundiata Keita, the founder of the Mali Empire?

And that he was born disabled, or so say the griots or West African singers who narrate the story of his life?

Sundiata Keita's father was Nare Maghann Konate, the ruler of Mali, a small kingdom in West Africa.

It was prophesied that if Konate married an ugly woman, he would beget a brilliant son who would rule the world.

So, Sogolon, one of the ugliest in the land, 'the buffalo woman', who, using her magic, had killed a giant buffalo that terrorized his kingdom, became Konate's second wife.

A hunchback and bent over, she may not have been everyone's idea of beauty but was possessed of such a wealth of kindness that it pleased the spirits.

'Even so,' say the griots, 'born to them soon was a son, one who was equally disabled.'

Named Sundiata (Sunjata) or 'the lion' by a loving father who saw not the disability but only the brilliance in his son, he was also the apple of his mother's eye.

However, he could only crawl for the first seven years of his life, till one day, tired of being mocked and ridiculed by his jealous stepmother and half-brothers, when called upon to pluck a leaf from a giant baobab tree, he heaved himself upon two iron rods, stood up straight and delivered to his mocking family the whole uprooted tree.

'Ever since,' laugh the griots, 'they humiliated him no more.'

Sadly, the king happened to die suddenly, and Sundiata's stepbrother Dankaran Touman was made king.

Thereupon began Sundiata's troubles.

Jealous of his popularity and scared that the people might prefer him to her own son, his stepmother, Queen Sassouma Berete, made his life a living hell.

When nine witches were sent to murder him, 'Enough is enough,' said his mother finally. 'We need to get away from here at once.' And so, they took themselves off across the border.

Crossing the River Niger, they lived in exile for seven years, wandering from place to place.

Facing untold dangers and numerous hostilities – even traps set by Sassouma Berete – they went from one kingdom to another till they reached King Moussa Tounkara of Mema.

●●●

In Tounkara, Sundiata found a mentor.

The king honed his warrior skills and groomed him to become a brave soldier.

Taken on military campaigns and taught fighting skills he wouldn't have known otherwise, Sundiata learned how to shoot straight and hold his own.

Intelligent and smart, he soon stunned them with his bravery and expertise, and was made Tounkara's commander-in-chief.

Then, one day, he bumped into some traders from his old hometown in Mali.

'Please come home, O Prince,' they told him. 'Soumaoro Kante, the evil sorcerer king, has captured all the kingdoms to the right and left of Mali, driven Dankaran Touman into exile and conquered us. Worse, he has taken your sister hostage.'

Sundiata was eager to go. 'Please, Tounkara, may I, with your blessings, go to liberate my people, the Mandinka?' he asked.

Tounkara, annoyed and afraid to lose Sundiata, said, 'No,' to a disappointed Sundiata.

Sadly, Sogolon fell ill around that time and passed away. So, Sundiata went to Tounkara again.

This time King Tounkara agreed, reluctantly, but also gave him half his army, as well.

Heading Tounkara's army, Sundiata quickly made for Mali.

King Soumaoro Kante, engaged in fighting elsewhere, sent his son Sosso Bala to stop him.

However, clever Sundiata planned his campaign in such a way that he took Sosso and his men by surprise, and routed his army. Sosso Bala managed to escape with his life.

●●●

Soumaoro Kante now took on Sundiata himself.

Again, Sundiata intelligently managed to get Soumaoro Kante's army in a stranglehold. He was about to put an arrow through Soumaoro Kante himself, when – using his magic skills – Kante hopped from place to place and disappeared from view.

Sundiata than gathered together all those against Soumaoro Kante and amassed a huge army on the banks of the River Niger, to make a major assault on Niani, the capital of Mali.

A massive battle was fought in Kirina, where Soumaoro Kante reappeared, heading an equally large army.

They were first evenly matched. However, soon Sundiata's men began to gain the upper hand.

As the battle turned against him, Soumaoro Kante tried to flee again.

Sundiata chased him till he again disappeared, but this time into a deep cavern, never to be seen again.

WHO WROTE IT AND WHY

No one single version exists and the epic was passed on orally from the thirteenth century (around 1217–55 CE) onwards by griots recounting the heroics of Mansa or Emperor Sunjata, until some nineteenth-century written Arabic summaries of *Sundiata: An Epic of Old Mali*, began to surface.

Leaderless, Kante's men surrendered.

Sundiata marched proudly into Niani to a joyous and rousing welcome.

Crowned 'Mansa' or 'King of Kings' of the Mandinka, he released all captured rulers and then brought them together under him, and began to rebuild and rule wisely. So wisely that soon Mali supposedly became the largest, wealthiest nation in the world.

'And thus began, with king after king paying homage to Sundiata, the Golden Age of the Mali Empire,' sing the griots, concluding their epic narration.

How do we know all this?

Balla Fasseke, Sundiata's own personal griot, gifted to him by his father, began to recount the glory of Sunjata or Sundiata, and soon other griots took up the narration to tell the world his story.

'Hakuna Matata', *the popular* Lion King *song by Elton John and Tim Rice, is Swahili (an East African language) for 'no worries'. More than three million people objected to Walt Disney being given a trademark for it. It was also said that* The Lion King *was inspired by a similar, popular Japanese animated story,* Kimba the White Lion.

THE EPIC OF MANAS

And then there was the hero who united the people of his country...

An international airport welcomes you in his name. A university bears his moniker. A mountain peak, why, even a planet, has been named after him. No festival or celebration is held without hailing him or recalling his brave exploits. Streets, parks, books, operas, movies and just about everything holds the memory of him.

Who is he?

He is Manas, the legendary larger-than-life hero of Kyrgyzstan and he has an entire epic, one of the longest in the world, dedicated to him.

For over a thousand years, the story of Manas has been sung, without musical accompaniments, by *manaschis* or singers of the epic. 'Manas sprung out of his mother's womb to land straight on his feet, clutching a clot of black blood in his right hand, which was how brave and unusual Turkic heroes were born,' insist the narrators.

'He was no ordinary Khan, this Manas,' they sing. 'He was a mix of gold and silver, risen on a moonlit night from the crest of a river and sprung from a space between the earth and the sky. His father Jakip, a shepherd, overwhelmed with joy at his son's birth, did immediately give him a foal called Toruchaar, which was to be his lifelong companion.'

Then the *Epic of Manas*, as it is known, goes on to describe Manas's heroic feats in bringing together all the people of Kyrgyz origin under one umbrella.

•••

Forced out of his home from Turkistan by the Chinese and the Mongols, Jakip and his wife had, along with many others, fled to a place called Altai in the mountains.

Praying hard for a child, Jakip had almost given up hope when they were suddenly blessed with Manas.

As it was foretold that Manas would recover their lost homeland, and Jakip certainly believed that prophecy, Manas set about trying to fulfil his father's wishes.

In his early years, Manas was a troublesome and mischievous teenager, but he was also generous and brave.

With his group of forty companions, he constantly annoyed the shepherds around them. He killed their lambs, and even as the shepherds went complaining to his father, cooked and hosted endless feasts to keep his group united and happy. He also taught his friends how to eat, play and fight as one. And he was soon directing and conducting daring raids into enemy land.

'Protected by the spirit of a black-striped tiger and a dragon, Manas, with a lion by his side and a black eagle flying above him,' boast the *manaschis*, 'knew no fear or terror.' Blessed with superhuman strength, a special divine sword and a spear that served him well, Manas with his band of forty men, who were by his side till his death, soon grew to be feared and admired.

As his popularity as a leader grew, 'Bring him dead or alive,' said the Mongol overlords, sending armed men to kill or capture him.

'No, you won't,' said Manas, who then single-handedly slayed and defeated them all.

Following it up by daringly venturing even further afield, he successfully began the recovery of his father's homeland.

Promising the various scattered tribes, 'You can keep all the cattle and other spoils of war if you fight and stay together,' he was soon able to win them over, and with their help defeated the Chinese and the Kalmyks of Central Asia in almost every battle.

Introducing them next to the idea of a unified Kyrgyzstan, he expanded his hold right across the hills and plains of Kazakhstan, China and inner Asia.

So much so that rulers from as far as Hindustan and Persia came to greet and hail him as a brave hero.

•••

Then one day, 'It's time you married,' said Jakip, and soon the beautiful Kanykei of the neighbouring kingdom of Bukhara became Manas's bride.

As courageous as she was beautiful, she soon bore a son called Semetai.

Manas was overjoyed but – alas! – away on his war campaigns, he never got to meet his newborn son.

For one sad day, in the midst of a battle, while his 40 companions were busy elsewhere, he paused alone by a spring to reflect happily on the news of the birth of his son. Just then, his enemy Kongurbai stealthily crept up behind him and hacked him with an axe dipped in poison, while another warrior let fly an arrow that struck Manas in his face.

Even as he lay dying, Manas told Almambet, his best friend and companion, 'Don't fight one another. May the stone that I made from a grain of sand remain a stone. May our people remain one people,' and asked to be buried in a place called Talas.

A distraught Kanykei fled the city with her little son and went home to Bukhara.

●●●

The *manaschi*s then turn to the story of Semetai and Kanykei, and recount how Semetai, as brave as his father, tried to avenge Manas's death and bring back the waning glory of his father's land.

Semetai married and begot a child called Seitek.

So, 'Manas,' chant the *manaschi*s, 'now lived through his grandson Seitek who was as brave as his father and grandfather.'

Further extolling the valour and the adventurous lives of both Semetai and Seitek, the *Epic of Manas,* a trilogy, ends with a *manaschi* reminder to listeners that it was, 'Manas who safeguarded our Turkic heritage and brought us together in this land that was restored by Seitek.'

WHO WROTE IT AND WHY

Sung by *manaschis*, *The Epic of Manas* is a compilation of Turkic/Kyrgyz heroic songs dating back probably to the ninth century CE or earlier. It was written down for the first time in the 1920s, filling seven volumes: the first three about Manas himself, his son and grandson, and the rest about his descendants. In 2013, the epic was officially included in the UNESCO List of Intangible Cultural Heritage of Humanity.

The epic continues with the narration of the acts of another five generations of Manas's descendants.

The number forty plays an important role in Kyrgyzstan. Manas had forty friends and now the Kyrgyz flag features forty rays of the Sun that represent the forty tribes that Manas first united under the umbrella of the first Kyrgyz state.

THE TALE OF THE HEIKE

And then there was in Japan, the rise and fall of a powerful samurai family...

In the Japan of the twelfth century lived the Heike or the Taira family.

The father was the head of his clan while the mother worked at the palace.

They were a samurai family and aristocratic warriors.

Into this family was soon born little Kiyomori.

Now, Kiyomori was no ordinary infant. He was a smart child, and he grew up to be a smart boy.

Before long, he became a smart man too. One to be reckoned with. One who couldn't be ignored.

So, one fateful day when his father died, Kiyomori assumed responsibility for the Heike or Taira clan. 'I am now head of this family,' he said, 'and you will all listen to me.'

He then got himself a job in Emperor Go-Shirakawa's court and soon rose through the ranks.

The Tairas, as you know, were a noble warrior clan.

So, across the country, wherever there was an uprising or rebellion, Kiyomori and his men were there to put it down.

Then Kiyomori made a smart move. He joined hands with Yoshitomo, the head of the Genji or Minamoto family, to quell what was known as the Hogen Rebellion.

The Minamoto was another equally powerful samurai warrior clan.

However, this Taira–Minamoto camaraderie was not to last. They were soon to fall out and become bitter enemies.

For, one day, when Kiyomori was away, the Minamoto clan rose up against Emperor Nijo and the retired emperor Go-Shirakawa.

Coming quickly to their rescue, Kiyomori suppressed the Minamoto rebels in the Heiji Rebellion.

Then, quick to take advantage of things, Kiyomori thought to himself, 'If I were to exile the rest, I can be in sole control.'

So, ruthlessly killing and exiling as many of the Minamoto clan as he could, he established himself as the sole commander-in-chief.

A grateful Go-Shirakawa also appointed Kiyomori the chief minister of the imperial court.

It made Kiyomori the de facto ruler of Japan.

The Minamoto family was not happy. They sought to hit back at the Tairas every which way they could.

This only made Kiyomori retaliate in every possible brutal way he could.

Thus began in earnest the acute hostility between the two powerful clans of Japan.

Then Kiyomori went one – brilliant – step further.

He persuaded Emperor Takakura, the son of the retired emperor Go-Shirakawa, to marry his daughter, and to them was born their first son, little Tokihito.

Thus, managing to consolidate his own position further, Kiyomori was now uncrowned king with all the unlimited powers of a crowned one.

Everyone should have been happy but nobody was.

This was because, unfortunately for Japan, Kiyomori the Taira warrior was an arrogant man. His cruelty knew no bounds and his ego was fragile. For every word or action against him, the penalties were harsh and cruel.

So, as he grew in power and pelf, so did his enemies.

Chuffed with his own importance, he also promoted his near and dear ones, and tried to, unsuccessfully though, even shift Japan's capital.

Fed up and angry at his cruel and conceited ways, Go-Shirakawa now began to conspire against him.

He sought out the Minamoto clan to help him curb Kiyomori. However, Kiyomori got to hear of the plot.

So, what did arrogant Kiyomori do?

He staged a coup.

He imprisoned Go-Shirakawa, and forced Emperor Takakura to abdicate and make his infant son Prince Tokihito his successor, who then became the little emperor, Antoku.

With his grandson now emperor, Kiyomori had even more unbridled power, and his ruthlessness knew no bounds.

He had temples burned down and gods condemned, people executed and whole families exiled.

However, whenever Kiyomori went on an execution spree, his son, Taira no Shigemori, tried to restrain his father.

He believed that his father's actions would destroy the family. He constantly prayed to God to make his father see sense. Kiyomori listened to him for a while, but sadly the boy died and Kiyomori reverted to his brutal self once more.

Kiyomori did not reckon with the massive anger and enmity that his actions caused among the people.

The Minamoto clan, in particular, believed it was their life's very mission to somehow bring him down.

Kiyomori reciprocated with equal if not more ferocity.

However, unknown to him, Prince Mochihito, the brother of Kiyomori's son-in-law Takakura, began to plot against the Tairas with Yoritomo, the exiled head of the Minamoto clan.

Battle scenes from *The Tale of Heike*, early 17th century

They had the active but secret support of Go-Shirakawa as well.

The hostility grew so dire that eventually the two clans went to war.

Known as the Genpei War, it would finally bring down the Taira clan.

On another front, another Minamoto cousin, Yoshinaka, also mounted an attack.

Soon there were uprisings everywhere and the Tairas were finding it very difficult to put them down.

In the midst of all this, Kiyomori fell sick. Suffering immensely, he died.

As he lay dying, it was said, Kiyomori's fever was so high that anyone who went close was burned by its heat.

However, the war he started carried on and large-scale battles were fought on sea and land.

Munemori, his son, now took over, but fate favoured the Minamoto clan and the Tairas found themselves hounded and defeated at every corner.

Yoritomo and Yoshinaka then fell out with each other as Yoshinaka tried to seize power for himself.

So Yoritomo sent his valiant brother Yoshitsune to put him down.

The Tairas tried to take advantage of the situation, but it was to no avail.

They were beaten back, executed and their decapitated heads paraded, even as they fled pillaging and burning

WHO WROTE IT AND WHY

Of unknown origin, the epic was supposedly composed during 1190–1221 CE, compiled into a single Japanese text by scholar Yukinaga in 1240 CE and recited by a blind priest Kakuichi – which was recorded in 1371 CE. Chanted to the accompaniment of the *biwa*, a four-stringed lute, by blind singers, the *Heike Monogatari*, meaning 'Tales of the Heike', narrates the actual historical enmity between the Taira (Heike) and Minamoto (Genji) families that engulfed Japan in the twelfth century, leading to a massive civil war on a scale never seen before, with Kiyomori, Yoshinaka and Yoshitsune as its main protagonists.

temples and villages behind them. They were finally and comprehensively defeated in the Battle of Dan-no-ura.

To escape being captured, Kiyomori's widow, holding her grandson, the young emperor Antoku, in her arms, jumped into the sea and was drowned.

Sadly, it was now the turn of Yoritomo and brave Yoshitsune to fall out.

Then, even as Japan was rocked by a tremendous earthquake and as every hated Taira was flushed out and killed, Yoritomo sent an army against Yoshitsune, forcing him to flee the capital.

However, Go-Shirakawa continued to support the Minamotos till his death, while Kiyomori's daughter, the mother of the dead little emperor, went on to live out her life quietly in a convent, till she ascended into her afterlife, states the Heike epic, bringing the story of the Heike–Genji clan to an end.

The epic starts and ends with the tolling of the bell, a significant Buddhist aspect denoting that pride will always go before a fall, as it was with Kiyomori of the Heike or Taira clan.

ORLANDO FURIOSO

When a French Roland turns into an Italian Orlando, his story becomes a very popular epic...

Want to treat yourself to a delightful jumble of characters and incidents?

Then, welcome to *Orlando Furioso,* where people fall in and out of love with one another, switch sides to fight a war, change religions on a whim and, most importantly, where dragons, magic weapons and sorceresses help them conquer and abet each other.

Meet Orlando, who is the Italian version of the brave French warrior Roland, nephew of Emperor Charlemagne of France.

Then meet Angelica of Cathay, with whom he was in love.

Next, say hello to Rinaldo his friend, who in turn hated and at other times was in love with Angelica too, and yes, do high-five Rinaldo's warrior sister Bradamante as well, who was in love with one Ruggiero.

A Ruggiero who, however, was an enemy and a Muslim Saracen warrior. Though raised by the Saracen wizard Atlante in Africa, Ruggiero defended Bradamante's honour against his own men. Then, to keep him safe and away from all the fighting, the wizard, who loved him greatly, hid him in an invisible castle atop a mountain, only to see him rescued by a determined Bradamante.

Now, Orlando was so in love with Angelica that he and Rinaldo fought over her, as did many others. She, however, was not in love with any of them, and time and again ran away from them all. When she finally fell in love with a Saracen called Medora, Orlando lost his mind, deserted his command post and went on a frenzied rampage around the world, destroying everything in sight.

•••

Ever heard of anyone's brains going missing?

Well, Orlando's did, and his wits were finally found in a bottle on the Moon by another knight called Astolfo, who ferried them back on a half-horse–half-bird flying animal called the Hippogriff.

Orlando took in a deep whiff of the contents of the magic bottle and lost consciousness. He then woke up, all bright-eyed and bushy-tailed with his brains intact, no longer in love with Angelica.

Instant epic magic?

Now, there were also two love- and hate-spouting fountains that Rinaldo and Angelica often drank from.

So, when they sipped from different fountains, they felt the opposite towards each other: while one felt love, the other felt hate.

However, when they both drank from the same fountain, they felt the same towards each other.

So, when they both finally drank from the same hate fountain instead of the love fountain, they fell out of love with each other.

Fascinating, isn't it?

●●●

Since they were in the middle of a war, Rinaldo then disappeared for a while. He was sent to England to fetch help from the emperor Charlemagne.

There was also a terribly dangerous Water Orc who captured poor Angelica who, as you know, was constantly on the run from her many suitors.

She was saved by Ruggiero who had himself just been rescued from that invisible mountain castle by – you guessed right! – Bradamante, using Angelica's magic ring.

Yes, there was this magic ring too, which made Angelica invisible whenever she needed to disappear.

If that was not all, Ruggiero fell prey to the evil sorceress Alcina's wiles and needed rescuing again. So, to his help came another sorceress, a good one called Melissa.

In the meanwhile, the Saracens led by Agramante, the king of Africa, were knocking on Charlemagne's French doors, in Paris.

Agramante wanted to avenge Charlemagne's earlier attack on his capital and the killing of his father.

So, he marched along with Marsilio, the king of Spain, Rodomante, another brave but arrogant Muslim warrior, and Ruggiero, straight into France.

You got it, the same Ruggiero, whom Bradamante was in love with.

Now, to be able to marry Bradamante, who was Christian, Ruggiero – a Muslim – would have to become a Christian too.

WHO WROTE IT AND WHY

Ludovico Ariosto wrote *Orlando Furioso* in 1516 CE in forty-six cantos and 38,736 lines as a sequel in Italian to the unfinished epic *Orlando Innamorato*, made famous by one Matteo Maria Boiardo. Continuing that story, Ariosto's *Orlando Furioso* or the 'Frenzy of Orlando' is one of the longest poems in Europe, glorifying romance, chivalry, patriotism, war and religion.

Ariosto was born in 1474 CE to the Commander of the Citadel, Niccolo Ariosto, of Ferrara, Italy. His father wanted him to study law, but Ariosto's interests veered towards poetry. He, however, took up a position at the Court of Ferrara and then worked for the cardinal of the church for a while before he went on to become a distinguished diplomat and then governor of a province in central Italy. Despite his eminent positions, he stayed a man of simple tastes and habits. He also managed to keep up with his writing and was soon regarded as one of the eminent poets of Renaissance Europe, a period in the fifteenth and sixteenth centuries when classical philosophy, literature and art were being rediscovered. He started *Orlando Furioso* in 1516 CE when he was in his thirties, followed by two revised versions in 1521 CE and 1532 CE, even while he composed other Latin poems, comedies and satires. He died in 1533 CE.

His other notable works: Five comedies: *Cassaria* (1508), *I suppositi* (1509), *Il negromante* (1520), *La lena* (1529) and *I studenti* (published posthumously); and seven satires.

The only problem was that it had been prophesied that if Ruggiero did that, he would die.

But then, the path of true love never was smooth and what was life without a few near-death adventures, right?

However, with town after town falling to them, Charlemagne's divisions were no match for the Saracens.

So, to Charlemagne's rescue came a revived Rinaldo back from England. He came home, took charge and managed to beat the Saracens back.

Orlando too – now with his brains back in his head after that magic whiff that cured him of his love for Angelica – and Astolfo went to Charlemagne's help.

Orlando then fought Agramante's forces, killed Agramante and ensured a well-earned Christian victory.

Ruggiero finally decided that even if he were to die, he loved Bradamante too much to give her up.

So, he stopped fighting Charlemagne's army, switched sides, converted to Christianity and married Bradamante, only to be accused of having turned traitor by Rodomante, his Saracen friend.

Confusion worse confounded, yes? Not to worry. It was all sorted out. Sooner than you'd think.

Ruggiero and Rodomante then fought and Ruggiero killed Rodomante.

He then watched Rodomante's spirit spiralling upwards, leaving the world, bringing this mind-bending epic to a sudden end.

Bradamante and Ruggiero are said to have started the family bloodline or dynasty called d'Este, and the poet Ariosto is believed to have worked for them. This bloodline is connected to almost all the European royal families of today.

THE SONG OF ROLAND

Leaving it too late to call for help, brave Roland falls victim to wicked Ganelon's treacherous plans...

'Please, sire, call off your men,' pleaded the messenger of the Saracen king Marsilla to Emperor Charlemagne of France. 'If you turn back now, my king promises you untold treasures, lavish gifts and hostages. He will also come to France and convert to Christianity.'

The Saracens were Muslims and were considered pagans by the Christians, and Charlemagne believed it was his duty to convert them to Christianity.

So, having captured the rest of Spain, the emperor's mighty armies were now poised to overrun the last Spanish city of Saragossa, and King Marsilla was now desperate.

Charlemagne pondered over the message for a while. He consulted with his men and his nephew.

'He could be bluffing,' said Roland, a brave and valiant warrior who was Charlemagne's sister's son and one of France's legendary heroes.

However, weary of fighting and tired of being far away from home for almost seven long years, they decided to accept the offer.

'So, who should go as our emissary to tell Marsilla that we accept his terms?' asked the emperor. 'If it is a trick, he will be killed.'

'Let my stepfather Ganelon go,' suggested Roland. 'He will be able to gauge the situation well.'

Ganelon glowered at Roland.

There was no love lost between the two of them. Ganelon hated and distrusted Roland.

He suspected that Roland wanted to see him killed and that was why he had suggested his name.

However, not to be accused of cowardice, Ganelon agreed to the plan.

So, saddling up his horse and leading a posse of men, away he went to meet Marsilla.

Reaching there, he decided to play traitor.

He suggested to Marsilla, 'We accept your offer. However, so long as Charlemagne's nephew is around, there will be no peace. So, while Charlemagne turns back to go home, you attack and ambush the rearguard with as many men as you can muster. They will all be under Roland's command.'

Marsilla listened attentively.

'Inflict as many casualties as you can,' Ganelon advised. 'Kill Roland, emerge victorious and win everlasting peace.'

Ganelon knew that Roland, not expecting an attack, would be unprepared and would not be able to withstand the onslaught of a massive move by Marsilla.

'You give me the keys to the city of Saragossa, and I will see to it that Charlemagne goes back home,' continued Ganelon.

Marsilla promptly agreed.

•••

So, laden with gifts, Ganelon returned to Charlemagne. 'Here are the keys to Saragossa. Marsilla has left the city with his men.'

A relieved Charlemagne made plans to return home.

Just as Ganelon had predicted, Roland took charge of the rear of Charlemagne's huge army.

Then the Saracens struck. They attacked the rearguard at a pass called Roncesvalles in the Pyrenees mountains.

Supported by just a handful of trusted men and his loyal friend and comrade-in-arms Oliver, Roland, knowing he had to protect the main army, decided to take them on himself.

Despite being surprised by this unexpected betrayal, they fought the Saracens, who were thrice their number, fiercely and quite successfully too, for a while.

However, soon Oliver knew they would need help. He begged Roland, not once but three times. 'Please sound the oliphant horn (made out of an elephant tusk), so that Charlemagne may hear it and come to our rescue,' he cried.

However, Roland, foolishly courageous and stupidly brave as he was, refused to do that.

He believed their little group could still win the day.

Alas, the Marsilla onslaught was so heavy that he was proved wrong.

One after the other, his men began to fall around him.

The fighting was brutal and as the corpses piled up, Roland realized he did indeed need help.

So, he finally blew the oliphant.

Charlemagne and his men heard it from far away.

Even as Ganelon tried to prevent them from going to Roland's help, the horn alerted the emperor that all was not well.

As Charlemagne made haste to his nephew's side, the call of the horn came a second time and a third time, even stronger than before.

Unable to hold out any longer and besieged on all sides, a desperate Roland, as if trying to make amends for

not calling for help earlier, was blowing the horn with all his might.

He blew with such great force that the veins in his forehead burst.

Chaos and confusion reigned as the Saracens sought to take advantage and pushed forward.

They managed to take back the gold and lavish gifts they had given Charlemagne.

In the melee, however, no one knew who was fighting whom.

Oliver, gravely injured, even smote Roland with his sword, thinking he was the enemy.

As Oliver also finally fell, a grievously wounded Roland, bleeding profusely and barely alive, took himself

WHO WROTE IT AND WHY

A Norman poet called Turoldus or Theroulde is said to have written the epic in French. *La Chanson de Roland* or 'The Song of Roland', composed in 4,002 verses, split into 298 poetic units called *laisses,* around 1040–1115 CE, is considered a popular French masterpiece promoting Christianity. It inspired many famous poets to recast the heroism of Roland in other languages.

off to a lonely spot on a hill, turned his face towards Spain, and breathed his last.

However, before that, he blew on his horn one last time.

The call was so weak, the emperor knew they would be too late to save him.

Brave Roland with the heart of a lion, however, knew that they wouldn't have died in vain.

His calls, he was sure, would warn the emperor of impending danger and help avenge more deaths.

And so it was.

Forewarned, Charlemagne's forces attacked the Saracens with such force that Marsilla was killed and the rest of the Saracen soldiers took to their heels.

Chased by the emperor's army, they ran, only to drown in a river nearby. And Saragossa was captured.

Taking Marsilla's wife as hostage, Charlemagne returned to France in triumph, but sadly, with Roland's and Oliver's bodies. The two were given a grand funeral and laid to rest as heroes.

Unhappily, Roland's beloved fiancée Aude dropped dead on receiving his body.

Ganelon's story, however, did not end there. Chained like a wild animal, he was tried in a court of law for betraying his country. Found guilty of treason, he was put to a horrendous death.

Thus ended the tale of Roland's last epic stand against the Saracens.

The epic is based on an actual 778 CE battle fought during Emperor Charlemagne's capture of Spain and has the presumed author's name in the last line ('Ci falt la geste que Turoldus declinet'), *though this is debated.*

THE METAMORPHOSES

When change is the only thing that is constant...

Metamorphoses. What does it even mean?

It's quite simple. It just means 'transformation'. And 'transformation' denotes 'change'.

So, want to know why ravens are black? Look no further than *The Metamorphoses*.

Once upon a time, all ravens were white. One day, however, while he was away, the god Apollo left his white-feathered raven to guard Coronis, whom he was madly in love with and who was expecting his child.

Unfortunately, Coronis was in love with someone else.

So, while Apollo was away, she went to meet her lover in secret.

When Apollo got back, the raven sneaked to him about it. An angered Apollo instantly – before he set out to kill Coronis – scorched the raven's wings for failing to guard her and for being the carrier of such bad news.

The raven turned black, and ever since, all ravens have been black. Thus, change happened.

Similarly, transformation took place when the world was created, and we went from chaos to order. It was followed by more change as we travelled from the Golden Age to the Silver and Bronze Ages, to the Age of Man or even further back in history.

And like the Diwali sweets or Christmas treats you love, *Metamorphoses* presents you with a witty array of some 250 tales from Greek and Roman mythology that are completely independent of each other but are linked together by a common theme called, you guessed it –transformation.

Thus, from the mythological story of a great flood that wiped out all human life except for a Greek couple named Deucalion and Pyrrha, who then created new human beings from the rocks thrown behind them, right up to the time Aeneas the Trojan hero, who fled Troy to lay the foundations of the Roman Empire, and Augustus who becomes the first Roman emperor, the theme is the same.

With flashbacks, and flashbacks within flashbacks, it humorously highlights the antics and adventures of most of our favourite Greek heroes, including Jason and Medea of the Golden Fleece, when 'change' occurred.

It was a transformation when ravens turned black for tattling, or the nymph Daphne changed into a laurel tree to avoid Apollo's love, or when Apollo lovingly wore the laurel wreath in his hair, or Mercury transformed a shepherd into a rock for betraying a secret. Let's go into that last story...

Battus was an old shepherd who discovered one of Mercury's many secrets. Mercury was the messenger of the gods, and a protector of thieves and frauds. He was also a clever trickster.

One day, he stole a herd of cows and hid them in a cave.

Battus saw it happen. So, Mercury made Battus promise never to ever tell on him. Battus swore he wouldn't.

Then to test him, Mercury changed form.

He turned into a young shepherd and cleverly enticed him. 'I will give you a gift of some strong cows, if you can tell me where to find some good cattle,' he said.

Poor unsuspecting Battus, forgetting his promise to Mercury, directed him to where Mercury had hidden the whole herd. Mercury now changed shape again, showed himself and, cursing Battus for betraying him, turned him into a stone.

Now take the story of Daedalus, a Greek architect. He attempted to change the order of nature by making man fly. He made wings of beeswax and feathers, stuck them on his son Icarus and himself and attempted to fly over the Aegean Sea.

'Don't fly too near the Sun,' Daedalus warned Icarus, 'the heat of the Sun might melt the wax.'

The Fall of Icarus, 17th century, Musée Antoine Vivenel, France

WHO WROTE IT AND WHY

The renowned Roman scholar–poet and orator Ovid, drawing upon every single great Greek and Roman poet such as Homer and Virgil before him, wrote the epic in 11,996 lines spread over fifteen books in Latin in the eighth century CE. Combining myth and history, he wittily explores the theme of *The Metamorphoses* in early Rome up to the reign of Augustus and after.

Publius Ovidius Naso, popularly known as Ovid, was born in 43 BCE in Sulmo, near Rome. Against his father's wishes, Ovid renounced his studies to travel around and, after trying his hand at various jobs, turned to writing poetry. He soon became part of an influential literary circle of well-known authors and poets. His early successes as a poet – his first poetry recital was when he was just eighteen – encouraged him to try his hand at writing on bolder and ambitious subjects such as those in *The Metamorphoses*. In a sudden turn of events, in 8 CE, despite his immense popularity, Ovid was banished from Rome by Emperor Augustus for reasons unknown. He continued to write until his death around 17–18 CE.

His other notable works: *Heroides* ('Heroines'), a set of imaginary letters from legendary heroines); *Amores* (The Loves), a five-book collection on love; *Fasti*, a six-book poem on the Roman calendar; and *Tristia*, autobiographical letters written during his time in exile.

However, Icarus flew too high, the wax melted and he was drowned while Daedalus himself, heartbroken, survived.

Change happened again.

Similarly, every story in *The Metamorphoses* tells us that everything in the world transforms or changes from one shape or form into another, in time. It could be physical or mental, huge or – sometimes – even minor.

And the nicest part is that you can choose whatever story you want from wherever in the epic, since it has no plot or storyline except for this single thread of continual transformation that brilliantly holds it all together. With no single hero, it is considered a 'mock' epic.

Ovid, who is said to have greatly influenced later Western patrons and practitioners of art and literature, including Shakespeare, continued to write in praise of Augustus even during his exile in Tomis on the Black Sea but in vain.

THE ICELANDIC SAGAS

Epics in prose are what sagas are to an Icelander…

Around the year 900 was when most kings of Norway, Ireland and Scotland were tyrannical or dictatorial.

Among the many Vikings or Norsemen, now known as Scandinavians, who tried to escape these monarchs was Floki Vilgeroarson.

And gently touching the Arctic Circle at a little island called Grimsey near Greenland on the Atlantic was a place like no other.

Floki Vilgeroarson arrived there, liked what he saw, decided to stay and named the place Iceland.

Shortly after, another Norseman, Ingolfur Arnarsons, a Norwegian chieftain, followed suit, and so did many others.

Soon Iceland's present capital, Reykjavik was born.

The winters were long, dark and dreary in this new place, and there was nothing much to do to keep themselves occupied.

So, what did they do?

They took to writing.

They wrote about their families. They wrote about their land, their legends, their explorations, their history.

Spicing it up with imaginative details, they narrated extraordinary tales about ordinary people and not-so-ordinary folks.

They penned tales about love, valour and honour, and revenge so gory that they even put in some witchcraft and ghosts.

Long and rambling, these tales soon became never-ending narratives.

They called them, you guessed right, sagas, and they were all in prose.

The poets, not to be left behind, had their say too in what were affectionately called 'Eddas' or `great-grandmother's tales', long poems of gods and heroes.

Some 40-odd sagas and an equal number of Eddas have survived to tell us the tale, giving us a more than an enjoyable glimpse into the incredible lives of these Icelanders who lived in the Medieval Ages.

So, when Erik the Red was banished from Iceland for a murder he committed, he sailed west only to discover Greenland and that became *Erik the Red Saga* and the *Greenlander's Saga*. His son, Leif Ericson, discovered America and Canada sometime in the tenth century. Written hundreds of years before Columbus discovered the Americas, the sagas describe the land as well as the lives of Native Americans with a great many entertaining tidbits, to become known all together as the *Vinland Sagas*.

Outlawed for having killed a man as a young boy, running from his enemies and slaying monsters with an inherited sword, the life of a medieval outlaw, replete with enough sorcery, revenge and trolls to make your hair stand on end, is the astounding *Grettir's Saga*.

Egil Skallagrimsson could, even as a three-year-old, ride a horse to a party and even recite poetry – and if you can believe that, so could the Icelanders who thoroughly enjoyed such flights of fantasy. Battling Erik Bloodaxe, his enemy, whose wife had witch-like powers, and tracing the family history from Egil's grandfather to his own children (850–1000 CE) is the literary masterpiece, *Egil's Saga*.

The deadly rivalry between two Icelandic poets, Gunnlaugr Ormstunga and Hrafn Onundarson, and their love for Egill Skallagrimsson's granddaughter Helga plus the duel they fought, which ended in the killing of one and the crippling of the other, make up the plot of the fantastic *Gunnlaugs Saga*.

Gunnar of Hlioarendi, a daring Icelandic hero who could jump twice his height in full armour, and Njal Thorgeirsson, a politician, lawyer, farmer and sage rolled into one, plotted to take over their district in the south of Iceland. Their opponent was Moror Valgarosson, the

local chieftain. Their adventures, full of wit and humour and not without the Viking special – blood-curdling kills and spills – can be found in the very popular *Njals Saga*.

Leading an army to unsuccessfully conquer England, wrestling with a giant snake and finally dying in a snake pit, Ragnar, the son of the Swedish King Sigurd, was a national hero. His exceedingly brave and able three sons, interestingly called Ivar the Boneless, Bjorn Ironside and Sigurd Snake-in-the-Eye, with their own stories to tell, accompanied by serpents, dragons, curses, witches, potions, magic and charms, make up *The Saga of Ragnar Lodbrok* and *The Tale of Ragnar's Sons*. They also figure in the Eddas.

Descended from the Viking god Odin, the story of the Volsunga clan, along with the magic of the Balmung sword, Fafnir – the greedy dwarf-turned-dragon, and the heroic tale of Sigmund who avenges his family's death and honour is as spine-chilling and fantasy-filled as they come. This is the famous *Volsunga Saga*.

WHO WROTE THEM AND WHY?

No one knows exactly who wrote these sagas and Eddas, but there are a few acknowledged authors like Sturla Thordarson, Snorri Sturluson (*Heimskringla*, a collection of Kings' Sagas) in Norse or Icelandic during the tenth and thirteenth centuries. Spread over three main themes, historical (*Egil's Saga*), mythical (*Grettir's Saga*) and romantic (*Gunnlaugs Saga*) they were initially all orally narrated by *skald*s or narrators to while away the long winter nights.

Detailing the struggle between the chieftains and the farmers through the rags-to-riches life of the duelling and temple-owning Hrafnkels who avenges his early humiliation and becomes a peace-loving leader, is the *Hrafnkels Saga*.

Secular histories can be found aplenty with *The Icelanders' Saga* leading the pack, in the collection titled *Sturlunga Saga*.

Delving further into Iceland's early history since its inception (870–1118 CE) is Ari Þorgilsson's *Islendingabok* or 'The Book of the Icelanders', which still survives and is widely read.

Now for the Eddas, like the *Voluspa* ('The Song of the Seeress') and *Voluspa hin Skamma*, which poetically tell us about various Viking gods and their fates, *Rigsthula* the comical and witty story of Heimdall the god who travels to Earth in disguise and interacts with humans, and Saemunt the Wise's *Elder Edda*, a tranche of 33 mythical and heroic poems.

These are but a few among the best that medieval Icelanders have created. If they don't make you cry and laugh or shake your head in amazement, it is said, nothing ever will.

And to this day, believe it or not, Icelanders read more books and even write more books than any other nation in the world.

Many sagas are lost to us because it is said that people, when they went hungry, would eat whatever pages they had written on.

POPOL VUH

'...This is the root of the ancient word of this place called Quiché.'
– from Popol Vuh *(Sam Colop edition)*

Nope, it has nothing whatsoever to do with the Harry Potter world or an edible quiche.

They are, in fact, the opening lines of the famous Mayan epic *Popol Vuh* or 'Book of the Community' in classical Quiché or K'iché, a Mayan language used in ancient Guatemala (in South America).

Using the Latin script and a Spanish writing system, the manuscript came to light through a group of sixteenth-century priests.

Various gods combine with deities, feathered water-borne serpents and other strange godly creatures, some known as 'hearts of heaven', in the still darkness of the night. Why?

To create 'Man.'

They first created man from mud. But unhappy with it, they then made him out of wood.

Still not happy, they destroyed what they made, only to have all the men in wood turn into monkeys.

They finally arrived at four real or actual men who were created out of…guess what?

Maize – with bodies made of white and yellow corn.

Wives too then came into being.

However, before that the rivers, mountains and the animals had already been laid out.

Then, in between there were two sets of twin boys who played ball games with the gods in the underworld and were killed, but one set was reborn as the Hero Twins, and their fascinating story is unravelled.

They attained special superhuman powers and turned into the Sun and the Moon.

And from all of them were descended various tribes and rulers that peopled their land.

In four parts, the *Popol Vuh* narrates:

- The Mayan myth of creation,
- The stories of the boys, the Hero twins,
- The origin of the Quiche nation, and
- Its history with Mayan rulers right up to 1550.

WHO WROTE IT AND WHY

Why is this epic important? The Mayans had one of the greatest and most advanced civilizations of the Western world. Attributed to unknown sources, it was translated from Mayan hieroglyphics, sometime in the eighteenth century, by a Dominican priest, Father Ximenez. It was then discovered by Adrian Recinos, a Guatemalan historian and scholar of Mayan culture in 1941, who published the first direct edition. The *Popol Vuh* is one of the oldest Mesoamerican documents of the early Americas.

The Popol Vuh *are handwritten folding books of long strips of foldable paper with a series of images from the bark of the fig tree called Hunn and known as the Mayan 'codex' (plural 'codices'). Codex is derived from the Latin word 'caudex' meaning 'trunk of a tree'.*

BYLINA

Nobody knows who composed them. Nobody knows who narrated them first. They, however, made their epic presence felt sometime around the tenth century and have been around in Russia probably even earlier but definitely ever since. Long or short, myth or fantasy, they are tales so fabulous that they will lift up your spirits.

So come meet the swashbuckling heroes known as Bogatyrs or the mighty female warriors called Polenitsas, and enjoy the fantastic miracles they wrought, and more.

Bogatyrs not only tackled giants and dragons but fought brilliantly for king and country while the Polenitsas were not just beautiful but equally brave as well.

Where?

In poetic oral tales called Bylina (plural, Byliny) meaning 'that which was'. Initially they were also known as 'Starinas' or 'old ones'.

Ilya Muromets, Dobrynya Nikitich, Alyosha Popovich, Sadko and many other legendary heroes of Kiev and Novgorod not only slew three-headed dragons or horrid whistling half-bird–half-men such as the

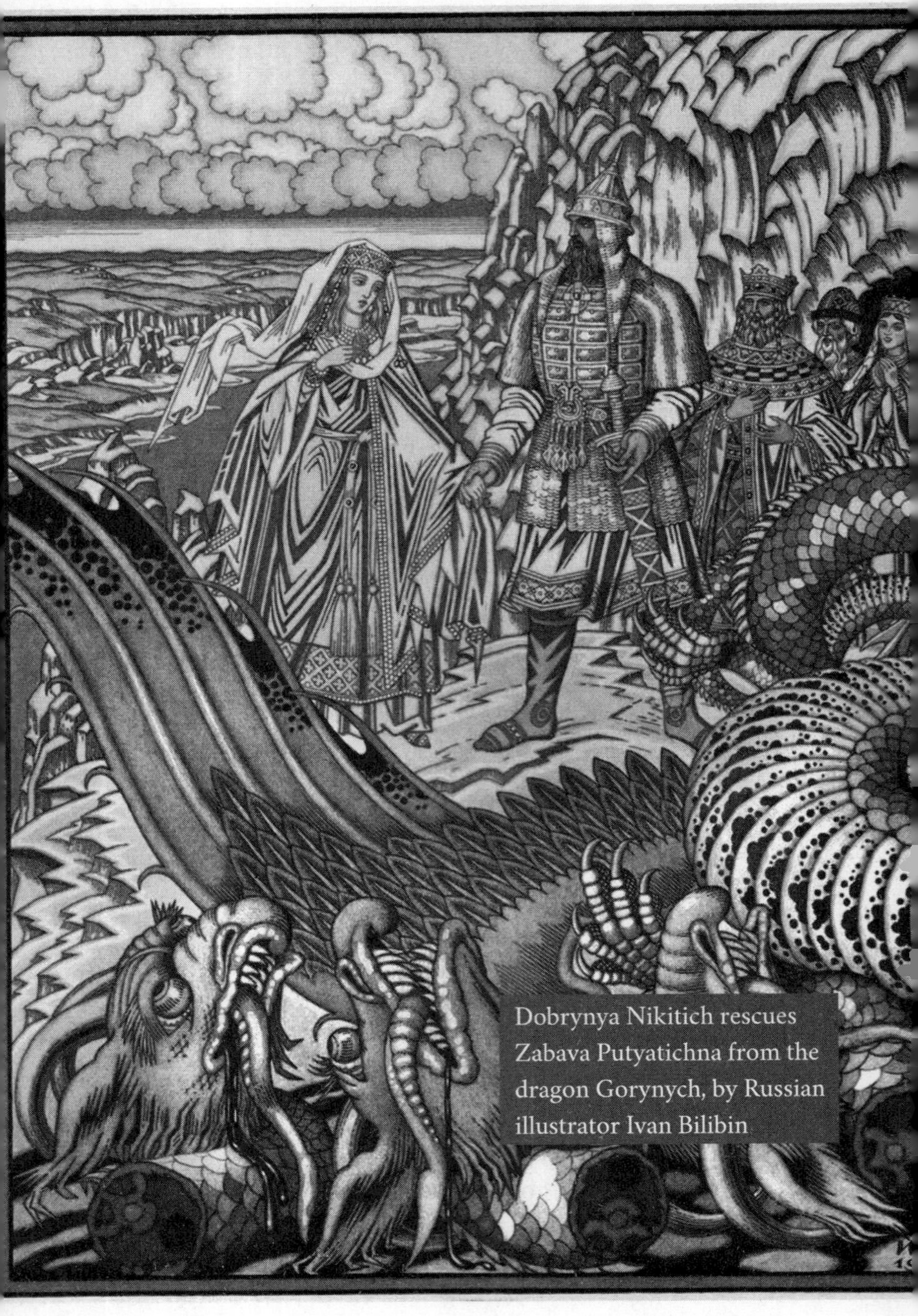

Dobrynya Nikitich rescues Zabava Putyatichna from the dragon Gorynych, by Russian illustrator Ivan Bilibin

Nightingale Robber, or won brides from under the sea but also defended their country from enemy attacks, predominantly during the golden reign of the famous Prince Vladimir of Kiev.

Told with great gusto to the accompaniment of an obsolete stringed instrument called the *gusli,* until they were all written down sometime in the 1740s and then published for the first time in 1804, these epic folktales – be they about Ivan the Terrible or Peter the Great or even the later Russian Revolution (*Tale of Lenin*) – have inspired and entertained Russians for a long, long time.

Dragons flew on wings of paper, and old heroes and giants could through their dying breaths simply pass their strength to younger ones. Imagine that!

ROBIN HOOD

'Robin Hood, Robin Hood riding through the glen,
Robin Hood, Robin Hood, with his band of men
Feared by the bad, loved by the good...'

...goes the popular song about a much-loved outlaw who became a legend.

Did Robin Hood really exist? Was there actually a band of Merry Men?

Nobody knows for sure.

However, fact or fiction, the adventures of Robin Hood and his escapades in Sherwood Forest are an inextricable part of British folklore, despite its lack of magic or mythological happenings. The magic lay in the devil-may-care attitude of Robin of Locksley who was constantly at odds with the Sheriff of Nottingham.

He took great delight in needling and taunting the sheriff and, while he was about it, never getting caught.

Loyal to King Richard the Lion Heart of England (twelfth century) who was away fighting the Crusades, Robin was not above showing his displeasure against the

Robin shoots with Sir Guy by Louis Rhead, an English-born American artist, illustrator and author (1857–1926)

regent King John (Richard's brother), who, along with the sheriff, laid a huge bounty on him for accidentally killing one of the king's men.

So, Robin, his Maid Marian and his band of men – Little John, Alan-a-Dale, Will Scarlet and others, led the sheriff and his men a merry dance by robbing the rich to pay the poor, showing up here and there and escaping, or rescuing his men from under the sheriff's very nose.

Often found breaking the law with mocking bravado, Robin's daring exploits turned a string of some thirty-eight oral ballads into a legendary epic (a fifteenth-century text). These folktales were then made into a novel in 1883 by children's author and illustrator Howard Pyle.

Robin Hood games or plays were performed as early as 1426 CE. Over the decades, many video games have evolved out of the tales. Check out 'The Legend of Sherwood', *a stealth-based real-time tactics video game or* 'Robin Hood – Sherwood Builders', *on Steam.*

THE TAIN

Epics aren't always about the solemn and serious. At least this one isn't. The Irish word 'tain' meaning 'raid' will have you enjoy a romp through the countryside of Ireland where two warring factions fight over – wait for it! – a bull, if you please.

Peeved that her husband King Ailill mac Mata had a white-horned magical bull called Finnbhennach and she didn't, the Connacht Queen Medb decided to steal Donn Cuailnge, the super-stud Brown Bull of Cooley, from neighbouring Ulster, whose people were unable to defend themselves due to a curse.

However, to Ulster and the Brown Bull's rescue came the dashing young demigod hero CuChulainn, who then led the queen and her men a merry dance.

Witches, curses, magic, divine intervention, supernatural heroics, duels, chariot battles, blood and gore followed when superhero CuChulainn blocked her every move, finally forcing her to retreat.

However, Medb managed to flee with the Brown Bull, which then went on a rampage throughout Ireland after,

CuChulainn in Battle by German–American illustrator Joseph Christian Leyendecker (1874–1951)

alas, killing King Ailill's white-horned bull, only to itself die later of sheer exhaustion.

Written in old Irish and set in old prehistoric first-century Ireland, the epic is enjoyably weird and full of life. A charming mix of prose and poetry, it belongs to a group of twelfth-century heroic tales and sagas called the *Ulster Cycle*. It is also Ireland's national epic.

Finnbhennach was born of Queen Medb's own herds, but the fertile super-bull felt that belonging to a woman was beneath him and so joined King Ailill's herds instead.

ARTHURIAN LEGENDS

King Arthur, Merlin, Excalibur, Camelot...these names give you a sense of thrill and excitement, don't they?

Though their tales do not make up an 'epic' in the strict sense of the word, they are nevertheless the kind of stories that legends, both magical and mythological, are made of. And so, if you have read them, you will agree that they qualify to be bracketed with the best of the epics.

First introduced to the literary world by Geoffrey of Monmouth, a cleric from Wales, around the twelfth century (1130 CE) through his *Historia Regum Britanniae* ('History of the Kings of Britain') with later add-ons by French poet Chretien de Troyes, the Arthurian legends soon became a part of British mythology.

Truth or fiction, the story of...

- the fifteen-year-old Arthur who pulled out Excalibur, an enchanted set-in-stone sword, to become king of England,
- the magic of the wizard Merlin, Arthur's adviser,
- the adventures of the Knights of Arthur's Round Table, who rode out to defend truth and justice, and

Arthur Leading the Charge at Mount Badon by English-borr. American artists George Wooliscroft Rhead and Louis Rhead

- the search for the Holy Grail (Jesus Christ's cup),

...are now all an inseparable part of British folklore.

The *Mabinogion*, which are early eleventh-century Welsh oral stories, also boast of Arthurian adventures.

There are many places in the UK, including Wales and Cornwall, that are linked to Camelot, Arthur's perfect court, where justice and honour prevailed, or Tintagel

While Camelot was probably situated in Wales, Tintagel is currently owned by King Charles III of England, as part of the Duchy of Cornwall properties he owns.

THE OSSIAN EPICS

Now for some epic fun.

James Macpherson, a Scottish poet, decided to perhaps fool the public.

He created an epic supposedly from Scottish oral traditions and some old third-century Gaelic manuscripts written by Ossian or Osin, a legendary Irish poet. And published them as actual translations.

The *Poems of Ossian* took the world by storm.

From French emperor Napoleon to the famous German poet Goethe and the French philosopher Voltaire, Osin's adventures of 'Fingal' and the later 'Temora' impressed eighteenth-century Europe.

They were translated into every possible European language with artworks, paintings and operas based on the characters in the Ossian epic becoming popular.

They also did wonders for the then growing idea of Scottish nationalism.

It was some time before people realized they may have well been taken for a ride. That perhaps the 'epic' collected from the Scottish Highlands was maybe just a figment of Macpherson's vivid imagination with some borrowings from Irish mythology.

What caused the suspicion?

It was the unusual mix of some actual and familiar Irish and Scottish legends, combined with some Homeric and Miltonic similarities, even a few Biblical tales, that made people wonder if these epics were mere translations of Macpherson's own eighteenth-century rehashed Gaelic poems.

However, at the time, there were also those who vouched for its genuineness.

Thus, though many today conclude it is indeed a hoax, the controversy over the authenticity over the real or not-so-real life and escapades of Ossian himself, King Fingal of southwest Scotland and his son Oscar, still lingers on.

For an epic that never was, the National Library of Scotland has an Ossian Collection of some 327 books and other items.

KHAMBA THOIBI

Manipur maybe a tiny little state in north-eastern India, but what is not small, however, is its large collection of brilliant Puya or archaic manuscripts. Among them is the famous epic *Khamba Thoibi Sheireng,* which is even longer than Valmiki's famous Ramayana.

What is it about?

It is a twelfth-century love story of Khamba of Khuman, the son of an officer, and Princess Thoibi, the niece of the king of Moirang (ancient Manipur). It was composed by the twentieth-century poet Hijam Anganghal of Samurou in 34,000 verses of 39,000 lines in the Meitei language. The Meitei language is a 3,500-year-old Sino-Tibetan language!

Spread over fifteen chapters and ninety-two sections, *Khamba Thoibi Sheireng* describes the endless troubles and misfortunes the young couple had to overcome (Khamba had to even capture a tiger!) to be able to finally be together... until one day, mistaking him for an intruder, she unfortunately kills him. After which, a grief-stricken Thoibi takes her own life as well.

It is an epic that is an integral part of Manipur's legendary folklore heritage.

A theatrical version of the tale is available on YouTube.

AL-SIRAH AL-HILALIYYAH

What is *Al-Sirah Al-Hilaliyyah*?

It is simply a long narrative in song that dwells on the adventures of the Bani Hilal Bedouin Arabs as they, around the tenth century, migrated or made their way slowly from Arabia to North Africa.

In about 100,000 lines, 'The Epic of Bani Hilal' or the *Al-Sirah Al-Hilaliyyah* ('The Life History of the Hilal') brings to life tales about the heroic antics of some larger-than-life heroes like Abu Zayd, who fought to unite all the Bedouins, and his rival El Zenaty Khalifa, usually to the accompaniment of the *rabab* (a type of flute) and a drum.

Once upon a time, this epic was part of all festivities and celebrations in the Middle East and always performed to music, but its performance is a dying art that is now found only in Egypt.

The tribe in North Africa was eventually overrun by inimical tribes from Morocco, which heralded their end. And from among what is left of the many Arabic epics

Abu Zayd al-Hilali (*right*) cuts off the head of Hegazi ibn Rafe, an old tattooing pattern, Egypt

that once existed, the *Al-Sirah Al-Hilaliyyah*, sung since the fourteenth century, is the only one that still narrates in the oral tradition the story of the lives, the heroics and the escapades of the Arabs.

Al-Sirah Al-Hilaliyyah *singers typically began their training early – when they were just four or five years old!*

RAGHUVAMSHA

Prepare to be surprised.

Lord Rama is proclaimed as one of the greatest of all kings. His father was Dasharatha.

Yes, you know that.

However, you didn't know, did you, that his great-grandfather, Dasharatha's grandfather, was King Raghu, whose kingdom not only stretched from present-day Assam to the Konkan down south but also up in the northern regions that included today's Iran, Afghanistan, Western China (Xinjiang) and parts of Central Asia (present-day eastern Uzbekistan, Tajikistan, southern Kazakhstan and southern Kyrgyzstan) as well?

Did you know that, even then, Afghanistan grew exquisite saffron, which got caught in the manes of King Raghu's posse of horses or that Persia was famous for its vine creepers and furs… and that there were and still are walnut trees in western China to which King Raghu's elephants were perhaps tied?

How do we know this?

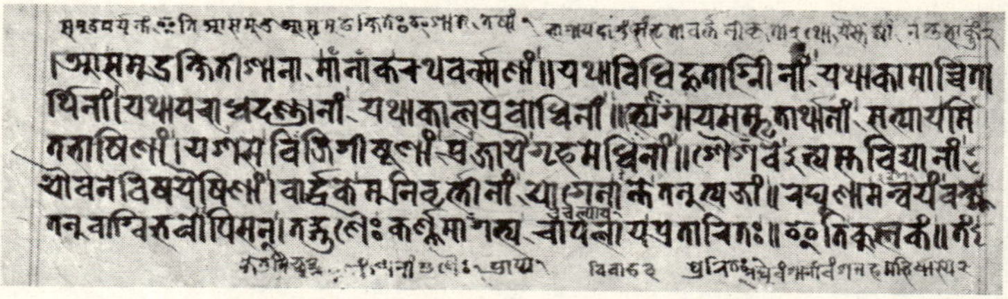

A copied page of the *Raghuvamsha* text

The great fifth-century Sanskrit poet Kalidasa's fascinating epic poem *Raghuvamsha* tells us all this and more.

Raghuvamsha or the 'Dynasty of Raghu', in nineteen cantos and 1,564 verses, is all about the reign and the grand exploits of the four kings before Rama and the twenty-four kings after him, including Kusha, his son who revived Ayodhya's lost glory, to finally close out King Raghu's dynasty with King Agnivarna, who had no successors. Along with *Kumarasambhavam* and *Meghaduta* ('The Cloud Messenger'), *Raghuvamsha* is one of Kalidasa's more famous *mahakavyas*.

King Raghu didn't know whether to go to Persia through the Thar desert with his army of men, horses and elephants, or opt for the easier sea route from the port of Kalyan. He chose the land route and came back a winner.

JIVAKA CHINTAMANI

Jivaka Chintamani, meaning 'Fabulous Gem', is the third of the 'Aimperumkappiyam' or the 'five large epics' of Tamil literature, the others being *Silappadikaram, Manimekalai, Valayapathi* and *Kundalakesi*.

This is the story of Jivaka Chintamani, a young orphan prince who grows up to avenge his father's death at the hands of the latter's minister. When the minister stages a treacherous coup against the king, the ruler, in an attempt to save his wife and unborn child's life, sadly loses his own.

Rescued by a kind merchant, the queen abandons her newborn child and becomes a nun. The child is brought up by the merchant.

Jivaka Chintamani grows up strong and brave, kind and generous. He excels in all the arts. He is an able warrior too, who overcomes his enemies one by one. He is popular wherever he goes. He even merrily marries some eight or nine times, and goes on to have a brood of sons.

He then accosts the man who overthrew his father, kills him and takes back the throne. A just ruler, he goes on to rule wisely till one day, tired of the life he leads, he gives it all up to become a Jain ascetic.

Spread over some thirteen cantos of 3,145 quatrains and written by a Jain sage Tiruttakkatevar from Madurai (in present-day Tamil Nadu) in the early tenth century, it soon reached epic status as one of the famous five great literary pieces of the Sangam period (300 BCE–300 CE), which is known for its brilliant literary output.

Tamil, which is among the oldest languages in the world, was found on inscriptions as far from India as Thailand and Egypt. More than half of the ancient inscriptions discovered by the Archaeological Survey of India in India are in Tamil.

VALAYAPATHI

Only fragments remain of *Valayapathi*, fourth of the five great Tamil classics (*Silappadikaram, Manimekalai, Jivaka Chintamani, Valayapathi* and *Kundalakesi*) of all time.

It is one you won't want to miss.

Likely to have been written almost certainly by a Jain sage, whose name is uncertain, it propagates various Jain principles. It tells you about non-violence and vegetarianism through the story of a young man called Valayapathi – probably a diamond merchant – who marries twice, abandons one wife and goes on to live happily with the other in another land.

Unfortunately, Valayapathi had a son by the first wife who pestered his mother about who his father was. The poor lady kept it secret for a long while, then finally blurted out the man's name. Off went the son to confront his father. Living contentedly with his other family and children, the man initially refused to acknowledge the boy.

So, to the rescue of the abandoned son came a goddess and soon the father was made to realize his responsibilities. Father and son were reunited. The father even set him up in a business when he grew up.

Praised for its great literary quality in various other literary works too, only seventy-two verses of the ninth-century palm-leaf manuscripts of this epic have been recovered.

So why is this epic considered great?

For its brilliant use of language and the sheer beauty of its poetic description: the culture and grandeur of the period shine through.

In the nineteenth century, a well-known Tamil scholar saw the Valayapathi's *palm-leaf manuscript in his teacher's library. When he went looking for it later, it had disappeared. The mystery of the missing manuscript is still an unsolved mystery.*

KUNDALAKESI

Imagine you are a young girl who falls in love with a thief who is about to be executed.

You beg your wealthy father to rescue him.

Your father loves you, so to please you, he pays an enormous amount to the king's treasury and gets him released.

You marry him. Live happily together. Till one day, when you jokingly refer to him as a thief, he angrily tricks you into climbing a hill with him and threatens to push you off and kill you.

What do you do? Shocked, you plead and beg for your life. However, when that fails, you do not panic but lovingly ask him if you could show him one last sign of respect by going around him and bowing before him.

He agrees and as you circle him and are behind him, you give him a massive push from the back. With no time to react, he tumbles over, falls off the cliff and dies.

This then, is the story of the famous Tamil epic *Kundalakesi* or the 'Girl with the Curly Hair'.

It is one of five great Tamil epics (the other four being *Silappadikaram, Manimekalai, Jivaka Chintamani* and *Valayapathi*) of the ancient Sangam period and is based in the town of Puhar in today's Tamil Nadu.

Thereafter, Kundalakesi, full of remorse for having killed her husband, turned to religion. She repented, became a Buddhist nun and went around spreading the Buddha's teachings. Only nineteen brilliant verses of the original ninety-nine have survived and is supposed to have been written sometime around the fifth century by a Buddhist poet, Natakuptanar. The recovered verses suggest that this is probably what happened before Kundalakesi turned to Buddhism.

Kundalakesi's father paid with, it is said, the thief's weight in gold and eighty-one elephants, to get him released.

BHATTIKAVYA

Could you convert dry grammar rules into enchanting poetry?

You could, if you were a great poet like Bhatti.

He not only based his epic poem *Bhattikavya* on the famous Sanskrit grammarian Panini's grammar book *Ashtadhyaya*, but he also went ahead and, in elegant Sanskrit, retold the entire Ramayana, using every single poetic technique he could think of.

Called *Ravanavadha* or 'The Killing of Ravana' as well, the *Bhattikavya* describes the various rules of grammar, moods, tenses and usages in about twenty-two cantos and 1,650 verses, divided into four sections, through the story of Rama.

Considered to be the next best *mahakavya* after Kalidasa's *Kumarasambhavam* and *Raghuvamsha*, the *Bhattikavya* imaginatively teaches you the rules of Sanskrit grammar and language even as it lyrically describes the beauty of its setting, sunrises, sunsets, the oceans, mountains, seasons and the rest of nature along with, yes, you guessed it, the lives of Rama and Sita.

So now you know why it became one of the most popular textbook-poems of its time, the seventh century.

An elephant decided to join Bhatti's outdoor grammar class one day. Even though it soon ambled away, due to this interruption, classes were officially cancelled for a long while. So, it is said, Bhatti got around the cancellation by composing the rules poetically and teaching his students without textbooks. And thus, was born his Bhattikavya.

SHISHUPALA VADHA

Shishupala, the king of Chedi, was a sworn enemy of Lord Krishna.

He was a great friend of Prince Rukmi of Vidarbha, who wanted his sister Rukmini to marry Shishupala.

However, Rukmini considered Shishupala evil and went away with Krishna instead on the morning of her wedding to Shishupala.

It was just one of the many reasons why Shishupala hated Krishna and found every excuse to try and insult him.

Now Narada Muni, the travelling sage, on one of his visits, reminded Krishna that Shishupala was actually an evil demon reborn and that it was Krishna's duty to get rid of him.

Although Krishna's brother Balarama told him to declare war on Shishupala immediately, it was decided that a one-on-one fight between the two was better than an all-out war that might involve other kings and allies.

Meanwhile, Yudhishthira the Pandava prince, sent out invitations for a great yagna at Indraprastha. Shishupala was to attend it.

Krishna kills Shishupala, unknown artist, British Museum

So, Krishna with his army in preparedness, decided to attend it as well.

As expected, the moment Shishupala saw Krishna, he started denouncing him as 'a cheat, a trickster who lies and deceives people', and when Krishna, who bore it all patiently, was honoured by the court, Shishupala left in a huff.

Soon after, they went to war and both armies fought it out till finally Krishna let fly the Sudarshana Chakra and beheaded Shishupala, thus bringing to an end Shishupala's sorry life.

This story is told in *Shishupala Vadha* or 'The Killing of Shishupala', an epic poem in twenty cantos of about 1,800 highly descriptive Sanskrit stanzas by Magha, a seventh-century poet.

It soon became one of the *mahakavya* that was applauded for not so much its storyline as for its dynamic and original use of language.

With clever adjectives and verses with double meanings, a play on words that could be read clockwise, anticlockwise or diagonally like in the spokes of a wheel, it is said to contain every word in the Sanskrit language.

Using just four consonants, the poet, for example, says, 'Sri Krishna who grants every boon, who is the curse of the evil-minded, whose arms can destroy the wicked who cause others to suffer, and is the purifier, shot his pain-causing arrow at the enemy.'
'दाददोदुद्दुद्दादीदाददोदूददीददोः ।
दुद्दादंददेदुद्देदादाददददोऽददः ॥
daadadoduddaduddaadeedaadadodoodadeedadoḥ
duddaadaṃdadadeduddedaadaadadadado'dadah'
(114/19)

KIRATARJUNIYA

'Declare war on the Kauravas now, Yudhishthira,' said Draupadi to her husband. 'Break your agreement. Do not remain in exile any longer.'

'Yes,' nodded Bhima, 'I agree.' However, Yudhishthira did not agree.

King Yudhishthira of Indraprastha, after having lost a game of dice to his Kaurava cousins of Hastinapur, was stripped of his kingdom, and with his wife and four Pandava brothers, Arjuna, Bhima, Nakul and Sahadeva, was living in exile for thirteen years in the forest.

Just then Sage Vyasa arrived. He had come to see how they were faring.

'Prepare yourselves for war when your exile ends,' said Vyasa. 'The Kauravas are strong. So, Arjuna, pray to Lord Indra and get some divine weapons from him.'

Arjuna therefore began to meditate on Lord Indra.

Indra appeared before him and told him that, under the circumstances, it was only Lord Shiva who could help him.

Arjuna, with the army of apsaras and *gandharvas*. Kangra watercolour, Himachal Pradesh, c. 1820

So, Arjuna then went to the forests of the Indrakiladri hills (in present-day Vijayawada in Andhra Pradesh) and began his penance to invoke Shiva.

Suddenly, in the midst of his penance, Arjuna spotted a boar. Just then, a *kirata* or a hill hunter also appeared. Both shot at it at the same time and the boar died. Now both claimed it as their kill and began to fight each other.

However hard he fought, Arjuna was unable to defeat and kill the hunter. Puzzled, he stopped.

'Could it be Shiva himself?' he wondered.

It was.

Pleased with Arjuna's warrior skills but, more than that, delighted by Arjuna's devotion, Shiva decided to show himself. He then blessed Arjuna and gave him what he wanted.

This combat between Arjuna and Lord Shiva, described in eighteen cantos, is the main theme of the sixth-century poet Bharavi's *mahakavya* titled *Kiratarjuniya*, or 'Of Arjuna and Kirata'.

Greatly appreciated for its highly descriptive and innovative use of the Sanskrit language, it is among the famous *mahakavyas*, which are in themselves mini epics, drawn from the Mahabharata.

The last verse in every canto includes a name or synonym of Goddess Lakshmi.

NAISHADHA CHARITA

'The Princess of Vidarbha is exquisitely beautiful,' said the lovely golden swan to handsome Nala, King of Nishadha.

'I shall release you,' replied the king who had captured the bird, 'if you go tell her about me.'

The released swan then flew across to Damayanti and told her all about the marvellously kind Nala.

And just like that, without either of them seeing each other, Nala and Damayanti fell in love.

With the swan acting as their messenger, they exchanged notes, and fell even deeper in love.

Her father then held a *swayamvara* and invited all eligible princes to attend.

Nala too was invited. Damayanti was delighted.

Among the eager suitors, however, were some gods – Indra, Agni, Yama and Varuna. They get Nala to try and persuade Damayanti to choose one from among them as her husband and not Nala himself.

Damayanti, however, was adamant. She would marry no one but Nala.

Damayanti before the five
Nalas, unknown artist

So then, all the gods turned up as Nala lookalikes and presented themselves before a confused Damayanti.

A smart Damayanti soon realized that the feet of all the Nalas, except for one, did not touch the ground. Sensing that was the Nala she was in love with, she garlanded him.

The gods, realizing their ploy had failed, revealed themselves, blessed the couple and departed.

On the way back to wherever they came from, the gods met another kindred spirit called Kali, who wanted to punish the couple for rejecting the gods. So, while Nala took Damayanti home and they began a blissful life together, and though the gods tried to dissuade him, Kali decided to hang around plotting their downfall.

The twelfth-century scholar–poet Sriharsha's *Naishadha Charita* narrates a part of the Nala–Damayanti story found in the Mahabharata. It is spread over twenty-two cantos, 2,800 verses and two parts.

With some superb imagery, and a poetic makeover, it turned out to be one of the most celebrated *mahakavya*s too.

Nala was a great cook. He wrote the first-ever cookery book, Paka Darpanam.

His Chitrapaka, an unusual recipe for ghee fried rice consisting of scented rice, onions, ginger, mushrooms, coriander, lemon, saffron and musk, eaten as is or mixed with meat, can be got along with other pre-Mahabharata recipes from his recipe collection.

SELECT BIBLIOGRAPHY

Sources that helped me bring the epics and classics to you:

Guerber, H.A.: *The Book Of The Epic: The World's Great Epics Told In Story,* Jefferson Publication, 2015.

Suso, Bamba and Kanute, Banna: *Sunjata,* Penguin Books, 1999.

Zimmerman, Helen (Trans.): *The Epic of Kings,* Wisehouse Classics, 2017.

Tusiani, Joseph: *Dante's Divine Comedy,* Legas Publishing Company, 2001.

Sutcliffe, Rosemary: *Beowulf: Dragonslayer,* Penguin Random House, 2016.

Homer: *The Iliad,* Maple Press, 2020.

Homer: *The Odyssey,* Maple Press, 2020.

Milton John: *Paradise Lost,* Fingerprint Books, 2018.

Tyler Royall (Trans.): *The Tale of the Heike,* Penguin Books, 2012.

Gyamco, Gyanpian and Wei, Wu: *King Gesar,* China Continental Press, 2011.

R. Parthasarathy (Trans.): *Cilappatikaram,* Penguin Books, 2004.

Internet sources.

IMAGE COPYRIGHT INFORMATION

Page 29: Michelangelo Caetani, 'Overview of the Divine Comedy', 1855: Wikimedia Commons Public Domain; **Page 48:** 'Siegfried and Kriemhild', published in 1914; Source: Baker, Emilie Kip. 1914. *Stories from Northern Myths*. New York: The Macmillan Company. Facing page 240: Wikimedia Commons Public Domain; **Pages 78–79:** Illustration: 'Prince Arthur, the Redcross Knight, and Una,' plate between pp. 144–145. From *The Faerie Queene,* London: 1751, by Edmund Spenser (c. 1552–1599); source: 63-2196, Houghton Library, Harvard University: Wikimedia Commons Public Domain; **Pages 86–87:** 'Rostam Kills the Turanian Hero Alkus with his Lance', Folio from the Jainesque Shahnama. Western India, c. 1425–1450. The David Collection: Wikimedia Commons Public Domain; **Pages 102–03:** 'Gesar of Ling riding a reindeer'; distemper painting; source: Wellcome Images, a website operated by Wellcome Trust, a global charitable foundation based in the United Kingdom; ibrary reference: Iconographic Collection 584928i; Photo number: L0040370; Full Bibliographic Record at: http://catalogue.wellcomelibrary.org/record=b1584928: Wikimedia Creative Commons Attribution 4.0 International license; **Page 134:** Illustration based on 'Batalla de Cuarte', Wikimedia Commons GNU Free Documentation License; **Pages 182–83:** *Clorinda attacks Tancredi* by Paolo Domenico Finoglia (1590–1645): Wikimedia Commons Public Domain; **Pages 204–05:** 'Battle scenes from the *Tale of Heike* (*Heike Monogatari*)'; source: Art Gallery of South Australia: Wikimedia Commons Public Domain; **Pages 226–27:** *The Fall of Icarus,* 17th century, Musée Antoine Vivenel, France; author: Wmpearl: Wikimedia Commons Public Domain; **Page 240:** *Dobrynya Nikitich rescues Zabava Putyatichna from the dragon Gorynych, by Ivan Bilibin*: Wikimedia Commons Public Domain; **Page 243:** Rhead, Louis. *'Bold Robin Hood and His Outlaw Band: Their Famous Exploits in Sherwood Forest'.* New York: Blue Ribbon Books, 1912: Wikimedia Commons Public Domain; **Page 246:** *Cú Chulainn in battle,* from T. W. Rolleston, *Myths & Legends of the Celtic Race,* 1911; illustration by J.C. Leyendecker: Wikimedia Commons Public Domain; **Page 249:** Rhead, George Wooliscroft & Louis. 'Arthur Leading the Charge at Mount Badon' from Tennyson, Alfred. Idylls of the King: Vivien, Elaine, Enid, Guinevere. New York: R. H. Russell, 1898; source: http://d.lib.rochester.edu/camelot/image/rhead-arthur-leading-the-charge-at-mount-badon: Wikimedia Commons Public Domain; **Page 256:** A tattooing pattern depicting Arab hero Abu Zayd al-Hilali (right) chopping off the head of Hegazi ibn Rafe' (left); source: Cairo Anthropological Museum (or the Ethnological Museum, affiliated with the Egyptian Geographic Society); author: Horemachet from Moskva, Russian Federation: Wikimedia Commons Public Domain; **Page 268:** 'Krishna kills Shishupala'; dated 1850; source: https://www.britishmuseum.org/collection/object/A_1993-0306-0-31: Wikimedia Commons Public Domain; **Page 271:** Arjuna and the celestials (maidens and accompanying musicians), folio from a Kirata-arjuna manuscript. Kangra painting; source: Los Angeles County Museum of Art, accession number M.70.38.1: Wikimedia Commons Public Domain; **Page 274:** Damayanti Choosing a Husband by Warwick Goble; Title: Indian myth and legend Year: 1913 (1910s); Authors: Mackenzie, Donald Alexander, 1873–1936; Publisher: London, Gresham; Contributing Library: Indiana University Digitizing Sponsor: Indiana University: Internet Archive Book Images @ Flickr Commons; No Restrictions.

ACKNOWLEDGEMENTS

Vatsala Kaul Banerjee – thank you for being the brilliant editor you are. But for you *Epicurious* would not have happened the way it has.

The Begum and the Dastan

Tarana Husain Khan is a writer and cultural historian. Her writings on the oral history, culture and the famed cuisine of the erstwhile princely state of Rampur have appeared in prominent publications such as *Scroll.in*, *Eaten* magazine, *The Wire*, *Al Jazeera* and in the anthologies *Desi Delicacies* (Pan Macmillan, India) and *Dastarkhwan: Food Writing from South Asia and Diaspora* (Beacon Books, UK). She hosts and curates a website on Rampur culture and oral history. She lives between Rampur and Nainital with her husband.

PRAISE FOR THE BOOK

Winner of KLF Fiction Book of the Year Award (2020–2021)

Shortlisted for SheThePeople Women Writer's Prize, 2021

'Straddling themes of gender and sectarianism, of royal autocracy and republican apathy, *The Begum and the Dastan* resurrects the lives of women behind the purdah, telling a moving, even tragic tale of pride, loss, courage and determination, as well as that unyielding human capacity to subvert tyranny through art and the power of stories.'

Manu Pillai, author of *The Ivory Throne* and *Rebel Sultans*

'Tarana Khan weaves a tale full of Razm, ishq, ayyari aur tilism, war, love, trickery and magic – and takes us on a fascinating journey into the life of a nineteenth-century Begum. The author's familiarity with the male-centric, feudal milieu and her meticulous research of the period brings to life a story of a woman and her story of love, loss and betrayal. The dastan with its use of two timelines keeps the reader in its grip throughout as it brings out the lives of a young girl in present times hearing the story of her ancestress.'

Rana Safvi, author of *Tears of the Begums* and *In Search of the Divine*

'A captivating novel that shows Tarana Khan's masterful insight into the human heart, complexities of love and tragedy. Framed through published and oral histories and dastans, the novel introduces Feroza Begum, a highly memorable heroine, through whose life we are pulled into the richly regimented life of the nineteenth-century Nawabi culture.'

Musharraf Ali Farooqi, author of *The Story of a Widow* and *Between Clay and Dust*

'Evocative writing that summons the soul of the feudal past, rich with history and romance and heartbreak.'

Namita Gokhale, author and Sahitya Akademi awardee, 2021

'A moving and affectionate account of a late 19th-century heroine, both shackled and emboldened by life in a North Indian court. The novel skillfully shows how the modern, in this colonial era, could take the form of a violent conservatism, especially in relation to women. The shattering and often cunning refashioning of women's lives is Tarana Husain Khan's fascinating subject.'

Anjum Hasan, author of *A Day in the Life*

'The story prompts the question: How can one write history without condoning it? In *The Begum and the Dastan,* history is an inspiration, a tool and an anchor, but it is not a justification.'

Scroll.in

'[Khan] has done an incredible job of combining fiction and history with a delicate hand of imagination. The story lives with you long after you have read it.'

The Daily Guardian

'Her novel sought to present historical fiction not from the perspective of the man as most dominant narratives do, but strived to represent the tale from the voice of female characters and their version of history. Khan ardently elaborated on the prejudices faced by women in the 19th century, the ones that women are still victims to today and the need for the rise of consciousness in these turbulent times.'

The Telegraph

'A magical realism journey into the old feudal nawabi culture weaving two eras… The magic of the novel will surely survive for long.'

Salman Khurshid, *The Wire*

'This is an immersive novel, remarkable for the thoroughly Muslim world it creates.'

Anil Menon, *The Hindu*

'With Feroza Begum, Khan seeks to examine how women thrust into this life of purdah, filled as much with glamour as with subversion, found the will to love and rebel, and sharply questions how far we have stepped out of similar oppressive structures in the present context.'

Firstpost

'…Khan accomplishes much: A flavour of Nawabi daily life, Rohilla military culture, the Sunni-Shia tensions mixed in with colonial influence, and, ultimately, the women representing each of these categories.'

Deccan Chronicle

'…rhythmic, mellifluous and near hypnotic quality of prose. Khan's smooth grafting of the flamboyance of Urdu Dastan to the Anglophone narrative lends Feroza Begum's tale a compelling power. It is an exquisitely rendered, splendid story which you can read at leisure. The book, indeed, is an unputdownable page-turner.'

The Book Review

'*The Begum and the Dastan* by Tarana Husain Khan has the ability to create enchantment with her words… Characters sparkle with such brilliance.'

Frontlist

'Document[s] the stories of women history forgot, who lived in Rampur and shaped the history of the town.'

SheThePeople

'...a haunting tale of a grand city and its women unfolding in three main narrative strands from the 19th century until the present.'

Desi Books

'This is a novel of parallels... Despite the glitz and the glamour, Khan's take on history remains unflinching.'

For Reading Addicts, UK

'Tarana Husain Khan is a master of imagery; her writing is imbued with elaborate descriptions of resplendent soirees, gloomy dungeons and busy bazaars that sweep you into the glamour and delusion of court life. Just as quickly, she will steer you through time and bring you face-to-face with the subversion of women's empowerment in present times... [Tarana] leaves her readers in a literary stupor, dizzy and yearning for more.'

The Daily Star

'[Tarana Husain Khan] herself had to go through archives, diaries, historical writings and, of course, oral history in order to tell the tale. In the book, the Begum's granddaughter tells the story to her granddaughter, making it through five generations.'

Moneycontrol

'This one's a gem for historical fiction readers with a passion for detail and atmosphere.'

GQ India